THE PRACTICE OF MEDICAL RADIESTHESIA

By the same Author

A RADIESTHETIC APPROACH TO HEALTH AND HOMOEOPATHY
or
HEALTH AND THE PENDULUM

AN INTRODUCTION TO MEDICAL RADIESTHESIA AND RADIONICS

THE PRACTICE OF MEDICAL RADIESTHESIA

by

VERNON D. WETHERED, B.Sc.

Second Edition with Additional Notes
by the Author

C. W. DANIEL CO. LTD.

60 MUSWELL ROAD,
LONDON, N.10

First published 1967
Revised edition 1977

© Vernon D. Wethered, 1967, 1977

SBN 85207 139 6

Printed in Great Britain by
The Camelot Press Ltd, Southampton

To
GEO. LAURENCE, L.R.C.P., F.R.C.S.Ed.,
devoted practitioner and pioneer
in medical radiesthesia

Contents

		Page
	Preface	9
1	The Homoeopathic Remedy	11
2	The Pendulum	15
3	The Rule	21
4	Samples and Witnesses	26
5	The Triangle	32
6	Testing with Radionic Instruments	38
7	The Psychic Factor	43
8	Some Factors in Case-Taking	50
9	Actual Cases	57
10	Radionics	90
11	Nuclear Fall-Out	96
12	Energy Levels in Elements and People	100
13	Diseases and Their Remedies	105
14	Organs and Their Remedies	119
15	Endocrine Glands and Vitamins	127
16	Miscellaneous Procedures	135
17	Conclusion	143
	Appendix	146
	Index following Addendum	149

Illustrations

Diagram: The Triangle · · · · · · · · · · · · · · · *page* 33

Vial connection between Delawarr instrument and 100cm. mark on rule · · · · · · · · · · · · · · · *facing page* 48

Triangle arrangement for testing patient's specimen against witnesses · · · · · · · · · · · · · · · *facing page* 49

Testing a patient's specimen on the triangle in conjunction with vial connection to instrument · · · *facing page* 49

Diagram: Dosage chart · · · · · · · · · · · · · · · *page* 56

Vial connection arrangement at 0cm. end of rule · · · *facing page* 64

Box of Turenne witnesses and other radiesthetic appliances · · · · · · · · · · · · · · · *facing page* 64

Testing a patient's specimen on the P polarity · · · *facing page* 65

Preface

My object in writing this book is to persuade medical practitioners and others engaged in the various fields of therapy not only to acquaint themselves with medical radiesthesia as a means of diagnosis and treatment of disease, but also to become active participants in the employment of radiesthetic techniques. There must be very many practitioners engaged in the healing art who, unknown to themselves, have sufficient sensitivity to use a pendulum and to carry out simple pendulum tests. If a practitioner has to decide which of two or more drugs will suit his patient best, the pendulum should ensure that his choice is the correct one.

An attraction of the pendulum is that it can be used to very definite advantage by practitioners with very little experience of it. As they become more adept in its use, they will find that its applications cover an ever widening field.

I have endeavoured to take the reader by easy stages through various tests and exercises with the pendulum, which he can try out for himself. Provided he has the patience and perseverance to get over the initial hurdle, to prove to himself that the pendulum will react responsively in his hand, it will not be long before he will find himself using it to an increasing extent.

It will become clear in what follows why it is that homoeopaths so often have a ready understanding of radiesthesia and make use of it in their practice. But I hope this will not deter the allopath. Radiesthesia can be employed just as usefully in allopathic medicine as in homoeopathy. Nevertheless, once the allopath has become familiar with the essentials of pendulum work for therapeutic purposes, he may feel inclined to experiment with drugs that are potentised. If he does this, he will find himself confronted with wide vistas of possible investigation, which should prove to be both interesting and profitable.

There is one point I should like to emphasise at the start. Not being a doctor, the treatment cases I have given in this book are intended simply to show how the different radiesthetic techniques can be applied. I have been studying the pendulum from the medical aspect for some thirty years and have naturally come to some very definite conclusions as to its scope in medical treatment. But in referring to actual cases, which was necessary for purposes of clarification, my object has been no more than to suggest directions in which the practitioner can develop his own ideas and assimilate radiesthesia into his practice.

This book, complete in itself, follows on naturally my previous work, *An Introduction to Medical Radiesthesia and Radionics*. This will explain the few general references I have made to the first book for the benefit of those who have read it.

I acknowledge my thanks to Dr. Geo. Laurence for his kindness in reading through my script, despite so much pressure on his time. As always, his counsel and support have been a great encouragement to me.

VERNON D. WETHERED

Weybridge

PREFACE TO THE SECOND EDITION

Since this book was first published I have adopted a few modifications in the techniques described. The most important of these has been the test for disease conditions. I have also employed new methods of test such as that for polarity in conjunction with the triangle. As time goes by the radiesthetist is always finding new methods of pendulum testing and modifying his work accordingly.

In this new edition of *The Practice of Medical Radiesthesia* I decided to leave the original text virtually untouched and to incorporate the results of my latest researches in an Addendum at the end of the book. In this way the reader can compare new suggestions for dealing with a problem with what has gone before.

During the last ten years I have become more convinced than ever of the advantages of radiesthetic and radionic therapies in the practice of medicine and the unrivalled efficiency of the homoeopathic remedy when rightly prescribed. I hope the new edition of this book will do something to widen interest in what might be described as The New Medicine and induce those engaged in medical work to study and benefit from what is a somewhat complex subject.

VERNON D. WETHERED

Weybridge, 1977

Chapter 1

The Homoeopathic Remedy

The number of people interested in medical radiesthesia is steadily growing. I have received letters from time to time from people in most parts of the world who have read one or other of my two previous books on medical radiesthesia, asking—and indeed sometimes pressing—me to give them more information on how to use the pendulum. But the subject is a complex one, and one can do little to satisfy the demands of a person new to the pendulum, by post.

In my first book, *A Radiesthetic Approach to Health and Homoeopathy* (or *Health and the Pendulum*), I gave a short introduction to the whole subject of human sensitivity as applied to the practice of medicine. My second book, *An Introduction to Medical Radiesthesia and Radionics* (referred to henceforth as *I.M.R.R.*), carried the subject very much further, and in it I gave a short survey of the radiesthetic and radionic techniques involved, at the same time attempting to show how our ideas as to the theory and practice of medicine are necessarily modified by the employment of these techniques. In particular I felt the need of impressing on the mind of the reader the importance of the homoeopathic remedy when chosen by radiesthetic or radionic means, and of discussing the way in which these means have modified, and to some extent supplanted, the method of classical homoeopathic prescribing. My opinion remains that the homoeopathic remedy is one of the most powerful therapeutic agents that we have, but that its neglect, and indeed its denigration, by the great majority of medical practitioners in the past has been due to the almost impossible task of prescribing it correctly.

Through the kindness of friends I have read several profound books on classical homoeopathy, often containing remarkable cures effected by homoeopathic physicians who appeared to have an almost uncanny grasp of the complex subject of homoeopathic Materia Medica. Indeed one sometimes felt that it must have been as much a matter of intuition as of knowledge that they were able to find just that one (and often rare) remedy which was apparently required to clear up a difficult case. Striking examples of cure through homoeopathy there have indeed been, but apart from the few specially gifted physicians who have had an initial aptitude and have given a life's work to the subject, it has been all too plain that the practice of homoeopathy through symptomatology, i.e. of classical homoeopathy, by any but the most expert, has all too often ended in failure.

I explained in my previous book how the potentised homoeopathic remedy fitted in ideally with radiesthesia and radionics, for in radiesthesia and radionics we are dealing with a force, a fundamental force in nature, and in the homoeopathic remedy we are dealing also with forces, with levels of energy which, when correctly applied, syntonise with energy levels in the human body. If sceptics of traditional homoeopathic practice could forget for a moment homoeopathy as practised in the past, depending on the matching of symptoms, and learn to find the remedy required by means of radiesthetic or radionic techniques, they could arrive at a completely new assessment of the value of homoeopathy. Those who have made a study of medical radiesthesia (by which term I include radionics), and tested it out in clinical cases, have convinced themselves of its value. They have proved to their own satisfaction that certain types of cases and conditions can be both diagnosed and treated radiesthetically far better and with more positive results than by orthodox methods. And yet it is extraordinarily difficult to convince the average medical man of the truth of this statement, if indeed he has any time at all to consider it.

The trend in a nationalised health service is all towards standardisation of treatment, of giving a name to the disease and then treating it by the book. The radiesthetic method is the very antithesis of this. As in homoeopathy, it presupposes an entirely individualistic approach. But whereas in classical homoeopathy the patient is treated as an individual through a correlation of all his symptoms, in radiesthesia the imbalances in his system are divined by a series of tests which may bring to light basic causes in the syndrome picture which cannot be revealed by orthodox methods.

Fortunately, private practice in British medicine is by no means dead, and for the sake of progress in medicine it is to be hoped that it will expand rather than contract. In the nature of things doctors in private practice can give their patients more time than is available for national health patients, and they are in a better position to explore methods of treatment of the more unorthodox kinds. It is amongst such doctors today where those employing radiesthetic and radionic techniques are to be found.

The question we must ask ourselves is how can an interest in medical radiesthesia be aroused in the medical profession at large, and more especially among private doctors, so that they can be induced to take a practical interest in it and indeed incorporate it in their practice? I think there are two answers to this question. The first is to convince the sympathetic, if still sceptical doctor, that he can use a pendulum himself, or indeed some other instrument involving human sensitivity. All too often a person being introduced to radiesthesia for the first time will say, 'Oh yes! This may be all right for some people, but I know I could never use a pendulum myself. I haven't the sensitivity.' The fact is that most people have some radiesthetic sensitivity, and many doctors could find useful employment for a pendulum if they would only give it a trial and persevere with it. Thus the tiro must be provided with a few simple tests requiring the minimum of equipment by which he can satisfy himself that he can use a pendulum. The next step is to convince him that he can really find out something worth while about his patients with this instrument.

The second answer then is this. The sympathetic doctor, once his interest has been kindled, must be persuaded that there are certain things that the radiesthetist can do for a patient which cannot be done in any other way. This is fundamental. While admitting that medical radiesthesia is still a very young science, any practitioner employing it knows that there are certain conditions which can be diagnosed and treated effectively by pendulum with completely satisfactory results, in a way which is impossible by orthodox means.

As an example of this I will mention aluminium poisoning. This is something quite definite and easily diagnosed by pendulum. As far as I know it can only be diagnosed through radiesthesia or some similar method employing human sensitivity, as it is not caused by finite particles of aluminium passing through the body, but by activated aluminium oxide. It is the activation of the aluminium which causes the trouble, and it can only be removed quickly and efficiently by a homoeopathic remedy in potency. The activation of the aluminium is matched by the potency of the drug. It is this matching of the activation of the disease by a suitably activated drug, i.e. a potentised homoeopathic remedy, which forms the basis of homoeopathic action.

I should modify what has been said by referring to radionic treatment, by which the activation of the aluminium can be neutralised by broadcasting to the patient on a suitable wavelength, but this is rather a technical problem which it is best to ignore for the present.

A friend of my family was suffering badly from haemorrhoids. All the doctor could advise was an operation. Eventually I was asked to carry out a radiesthetic test. I diagnosed acute aluminium poisoning. The lady was treated for this with appropriate remedies and persuaded to give up using aluminium cooking utensils. The trouble cleared up quite quickly and, as far as I know, she has never had any trouble in this direction since.

This is the sort of case by which a medical man could be persuaded of the value of radiesthesia. Unfortunately most cases are not as simple as this, several factors often being found, all contributing to the disease syndrome. Nevertheless, if chapter and verse could be given of cases in which one predominant cause was correctly diagnosed and effectively treated through radiesthesia, this might do much to convince the sceptic that, after all, medical radiesthesia has something very definite to offer, especially in difficult and unresolved cases where orthodox measures have failed. In the following chapters simple tests are described, which anyone should be able to follow, and suggestions are made as to how the practitioner can proceed in diagnosing and treating a case.

Chapter 2

The Pendulum

All radiesthetic tests depend on human sensitivity. The value of instruments such as the pendulum is that they give a clear indication of what the human reaction is. Some people with a high degree of sensitivity can dowse for water without any instrument at all. If it were possible to examine closely what happens when almost anybody walks across a stream band with arms extended in a forward direction, it would be found that the arms and hands vibrate slightly. If the person at the same time holds a pendulum in one hand, it will begin to gyrate, following the motion of the hand. Thus the pendulum interprets the signal received by the dowser. The pendulum is the most sensitive of all dowsing instruments and is especially suited to precise work of a laboratory nature, as is required in medical radiesthesia.

Most people can obtain pendulum reactions, but the beginner must be patient in his attempts to obtain one. It is important that he should have a pendulum which is suited to him and that he suspends it from his fingers with the correct length of thread. A small cotton reel makes a very good pendulum, suspended by a fairly flexible piece of thread or twine. Assuming that the beginner is right-handed, he should try holding the pendulum over a piece of white paper with, say, a 2-in. length of suspension, and then gradually allow the thread to slip through his fingers. There may come a point when the pendulum comes to life and begins to gyrate. This will probably happen with a suspension length of 4 to 6in. But even if he is disappointed with this little experiment, he should not be dispirited. He can repeat the experiment holding the pendulum over his left hand. He can also hold it over his thigh. He can hold it over various objects such as a torch battery or a wireless set, or even see if it reacts as he walks about the room. With it he should be able to trace the under-floor electric wiring.

A very good way of testing out the pendulum for the first time is to place half a dozen homoeopathic remedies on white pieces of paper in front of you on the table, preferably in 3x or 6c potencies, and find what happens to the pendulum when it is held over each in turn. Owing to the activation of the remedies through potentisation, they give out a relatively strong influence, which should be easily detected by most people. If the pendulum reacts strongly in a clockwise direction over one remedy, that remedy is probably well indicated for the person concerned. If it gyrates anti-clockwise, it is probably contra-indicated, whereas if the pendulum oscillates, we can assume that the remedy will have little effect either way. I should regard these reactions as normal, but some individuals may find that the interpretation of these reactions is reversed. Over underground water the pendulum will probably gyrate anti-clockwise. Each individual must check his reactions for himself.

Such testing should not be difficult as, instead of using remedies, he can test out varieties of food and drink. In this way he should soon know what his reactions mean. In the ordinary way one refers to a reaction where the food or other material agrees with the person, thus giving a clockwise reaction, as being positive, while an anti-clockwise reaction is negative. However, the late Captain W. H. Trinder, author of that excellent little book, *Dowsing*, and a very good exponent of the rod and pendulum, had opposite reactions. He also mentioned in his book that the late Abbé Mermet used to test the organs of a patient by holding his pendulum away from him and using the first finger of his free hand as a pointer. While gyrating for a healthy organ, the pendulum oscillated for one that was unhealthy.

Individual colours produce specific pendulum reactions. The colour red gives a positive reaction, while blue gives a negative one. Green is regarded radiesthetically as being neutral. The beginner can try his pendulum over these colours. He can of course also try it over ordinary medicines such as aspirin, cold cures, liver remedies, tonics and so on, and as his skill develops he should find simple tests like this of considerable value.

He can also find out whether a remedy suits some person other than himself. He can hold his pendulum over the palm of one hand of the person tested and then ask him to pick up in turn several remedies with the other hand. With a good remedy the pendulum should gyrate clockwise. He can make the pendulum gyrate over the remedy and then transfer it to the palm of the person's hand. If it continues to gyrate positively, it is well indicated. Or again, the remedy can be placed on the open palm of the person tested, whether it be that of the operator or someone else, and a clockwise gyration is a favourable indication. Another method is for the operator himself to pick up each remedy in turn as he holds his pendulum over the hand of someone else. There is really no limit to what can be done by simple tests of this nature, and it is for the individual to find out which method suits him best.

Having satisfied himself that the pendulum is responsive in his hands, the beginner can pass on to simple tests which can be carried out with the minimum of equipment. It is inevitable that in describing these tests, the author will be recapitulating to some extent methods he has described in his previous works. At the same time the present book is meant to deal only with objective tests, and not with a general discussion of the theories and philosophy underlying the whole practice of medical radiesthesia. For instance, in *I.M.R.R.* I endeavoured to show the part played by radiesthesia in the prescription of homoeopathic remedies and how some account should be taken of the classical method of prescribing as based on symptomatology. In other words a good practitioner would employ to the full both his knowledge of homoeopathic Materia Medica and his radiesthetic tests in finding the correct remedy, or remedies. The one system would confirm and amplify the other. No attempt will be made to go over this ground again.

Before embarking on serious work, it is just as well for the beginner to acquire two or three pendulums and discover which suits him best. He will probably find that in using a particular method, a particular pendulum will give best results. He may thus keep in use two or three pendulums, employing each one according to the method he is following at the time. I myself have constantly in use three pendulums, one for work on a rule, another for work on a triangle and still a third for deciding on dosage by mental orientation. All this will be discussed later.

Whale ivory pendulums are extensively used by radiesthetists, as are those made of plastic. The sort of pendulum I have found useful in general work is a whale ivory pendulum of pear shape, 3½cm. long by 2½cm. wide and weighing ⅜oz. The pendulums are generally of cavity type, i.e. they are hollow inside and have a screw-on cap. The idea of this is that if you are prospecting in the field for iron, for example, you place a small piece of iron inside the pendulum, and when you walk over a spot on the ground where the iron lies buried, the iron in the pendulum will syntonise with the iron in the ground; in other words a radiesthetic link will be set up between the two and the pendulum will react in the hands of the operator. We say then that the iron in the pendulum is used as a sample or 'witness' (after the French word *témoin*). Witnesses are used in many kinds of radiesthetic work. Actually it is generally better not to put the sample inside the pendulum, but to hold it against the string of the pendulum in the pendulum hand. The reason for this is that after the sample has been removed from the pendulum, and especially if it has been there for some time, its influence or radiation may remain for some time inside the cavity, thus vitiating further tests.

Whale ivory pendulums are often suspended by a thread attached at the other end to a small whale ivory stick or ring. Some people find a holder of this kind more convenient than just holding the thread between the fingers. In work on the rule, where one obtains readings by pendulum oscillations, I prefer a holder of the stick type, while for work in which the answer is given by gyrations of the pendulum, I personally favour the ring. For work in the field there is much to be said for a spherical pendulum, while a convenient pendulum for the pocket is an ivory bob, 2cm. in diameter and weighing ½oz. The thread passes through a hole drilled through the centre, and as the pendulum is free to pass to either end of the thread, it can be used either way up. This might conceivably be an advantage, as the pendulum may give rather better reactions one way up than the other. The reason for this is that some objects give different reactions at different points on their surface. One could say that they are 'polarised'. But this really does not concern us here. With a small spherical pendulum as described, the thread is held between the first finger and thumb. It is not necessary to use a rod or ring holder, and indeed any pendulum can be suspended from the first finger and thumb by the thread alone.

I once had the opportunity of demonstrating before a group of young doctors my own method of testing with a pendulum, a rule and a radionic instrument. Afterwards I was asked to allow these doctors to see if they could get any reaction when holding the pendulum over the rule. In the hands of one of these doctors the pendulum immediately began to gyrate violently and this occurred all along the rule. With practice he would have made a very good radiesthetist and, for all I know, he has become one by now. It can be a most exciting moment in one's life when one realises that one has obtained a dowsing reaction for the first time. And it often happens quite quickly. Down through the ages dowsers have been employed to find underground streams, especially in countries like India, where villages are often short of water. It is comparatively recently that dowsers have realised that underground streams can be a cause of ill-health and that it is best not to sleep immediately over such a stream.

Some people have been able to cure their insomnia or rheumatism, or whatever it may be, simply by moving their bed to a different position. Bad earth radiations affecting health can be caused by faults and fissures in the ground, and contaminated water may be very deleterious. It is extremely inadvisable to sleep over a spot where two underground streams cross each other.

It is not a difficult matter to go over a house with a pendulum and discover places where the pendulum turns anti-clockwise. Over a very bad spot it may become inert. A good deal of work has been done on earth rays on the Continent and evidence has been produced suggesting that they may be a cause of cancer. So the budding pendulist can employ his pendulum usefully at an early stage in carrying out prospections of this kind.

A certain amount of tact is implicit in this sort of work and it is obviously a mistake to worry people unnecessarily when there is no real need. Nevertheless there are times in illness, especially chronic illness, when the possibility of earth rays being a factor in the case should be considered. No person can remain well if he is spending much of his life immediately over a bad example of what the French call *ondes noçives*. The mere moving of a bed to a different position in a room may make all the difference.

It is strange that just as one can prospect a house or site with a pendulum, one can get equally good results by using a plan or sketch of the house. This is known as map-dowsing. One simply goes over the map carefully with a pendulum and finds any bad spots on it, just as one would if one was actually inside the house. I have carried out prospections on sketches of flats in South Africa, and the suggestions I was able to make as to repositioning a bed, for example, proved well worth while.

Just as one can find faults in the ground and places where the earth rays are harmful, so is it possible to use the pendulum for finding faults in human tissue or organs. If a person has something wrong with his spine, you can find out where the trouble is by getting him to lie face downwards on a couch and moving your pendulum slowly along his spine from the neck downwards. As a lesion is approached the pendulum will begin to turn anti-clockwise. Areas where fibrositis exists can be picked out in this way.

Radiesthetists know that the state of certain organs can be determined by holding a pendulum over the fingers of either the right or left hand. What has been called the 'General Polarity' is represented by the tip of the thumb. If you hold a pendulum with a fairly short suspension over either thumb, it will probably oscillate, but if the subject is in bad health, his general polarity will be affected and the pendulum will gyrate either clockwise or anti-clockwise. A clockwise gyration would probably mean that the subject was in a febrile or actively toxic condition.

A very simple test should convince any pendulist, however inexperienced, that the pendulum will detect damaged tissue. All he has to do is to hold his pendulum over his thigh and find out what his normal reaction is, and then slap his thigh fairly hard with the palm of the hand. His pendulum will then indicate damaged tissue, probably by an anti-clockwise gyration. If he continues to hold his pendulum over the damaged area, the time will come when the gyrations will begin to slow down and the pendulum will gradually return to a normal reaction, probably oscillations if the suspension length of the pendulum is reasonably short. When this occurs the effect of the slap has worn off and the tissue has become normal again.

Chapter 3

The Rule

Having found what he can do with a pendulum as his sole instrument, the beginner should next obtain a 100cm. rule. Any carpenter should be able to make one for him and the owner can mark it quite easily himself with a ball-point pen. The rule should be rather longer than 100cm., say 106cm. in all, so that there is a 3cm. overlap at each end of the 100cm. scale. A suitable width would be 3½cm., the depth being 1cm. The rule will ordinarily be placed on a table, and in order to insulate it from any stray radiesthetic influences on the table, it should be supported at each end by a rubber block. Additional blocks should be placed on either side alongside the rule at the 0cm. and 100cm. positions, so that drug and other samples can be placed on them.

If the reader will now support his rule on the blocks, preferably in an east-west direction, and place a sample of his saliva on the rule at 0cm., he will find that the pendulum balances at about 38–40cm. His saliva specimen is best obtained by spitting into a small glass vial. Personally I believe that all samples used on a rule should preferably be placed in a glass vial, as the vial acts as a resonance chamber and the radiesthetic influence is to that extent stronger. It may not be easy to find this balance point at first, but it can be found by most people with a little practice. Hold the pendulum over the rule and move the pendulum hand slowly from 0cm. up the rule. When it comes to the 38–40cm. band, you will probably feel a slight pull in the opposite direction. If this does not occur, repeat the experiment, but allow the pendulum to oscillate slowly across the rule as you move your hand. In order to pin-point the balance point, hold your pendulum over the 40cm. mark and allow it to oscillate slowly at right angles to the rule. It may tend to oscillate across the rule, but not quite at right angles. Move the pendulum slowly first down the rule, and then up. At one point, and at one point only (within the vicinity of the 40cm. mark), will it oscillate freely at exactly right angles. This is the balance point.

Supposing you want a tonic and are not sure as to which of two or three would suit you best. Hold one of the medicines in your left hand and see what effect this has on the pendulum balance point, your saliva specimen being positioned at 0cm. on the rule. You will probably find that it rises to some figure such as 45 or 50cm. The medicine producing the highest reading will be the one that suits you best. Instead of holding each medicine in turn in your free hand, you can if you like place it alongside your specimen, but just off the rule, on one of the rubber blocks. Such a test can of course equally be employed for testing the suitability of a medicine for someone else, with his saliva specimen placed at 0cm.

Radiesthetists know that there is a radiesthetic link between a person and his saliva specimen and that tests on that specimen will represent what is the state of that person at the moment of test. When you hold a medicine in your free hand and find the balance point on the rule with your own specimen at 0cm., you are measuring the effect the medicine would have on you because of the radiesthetic link between yourself and your saliva specimen.

In my book *I.M.R.R.* I described readings taken on the rule with only the saliva specimen of the patient on it (at 0cm.) as vitality or *R* (rule) readings. Medicine which agrees with a patient and is truly indicated will invariably increase his vitality and almost invariably increase the *R* reading. Homoeopathic remedies derive their effect very largely (except in the lowest potencies) from the energy produced in their potentisation, and that is why such clear indications can be obtained as to their suitability through radiesthetic tests. Not only that, but the potency required in a particular case can be determined.

Suppose, for instance, that Silica is chosen as a remedy to satisfy a case. If you put a vial of Silica 3x on the rubber block alongside the specimen of the patient (placed at 0cm. on the rule), the reading may go up from, say, 38cm. to 60cm. Silica 6 may take the reading up to 90cm. or over, while Silica 30 may only produce a reading of, say, 70cm. Silica 6 is then the obvious potency to employ. A suitable combination of remedies may take the reading up to 100cm. If that happens, the prescription should be a useful one. Often enough, with three remedies together giving a reading of 80cm. or over, the addition of another remedy, well indicated by itself, will reduce the reading, showing that it will not fit in with the other remedies. But it is found through radiesthesia that much more can often be achieved by combining two or more remedies, rather than employing one remedy only. This aspect of medical radiesthesia was fully discussed in my previous book.

A quick check for a prescription, where the patient's specimen is at 0cm. with the remedies grouped around it, is to let the pendulum oscillate across the rule at 100cm. Then slowly move the pendulum down the rule, and if you feel a resistance and the pendulum balances at anything over 97cm., the prescription is a good one. With a really good prescription the pendulum will balance at 100cm. and even slightly above it. I should, however, point out that I am left-handed myself and right-handed pendulists may have to find their own precise balance points.

It will be apparent from the foregoing that you can, with only a pendulum and a rule, check both the suitability and potency of a drug for a given individual. A really first-class remedy will take the pendulum right up the scale to 80cm. or over. You can also make a *direct* check as to suitability by asking the patient to hold the remedies in one hand and then hold the pendulum over the other, palm upwards. If the pendulum gyrates clockwise, the prescription is a good one.

The practitioner will soon discover what is the normal R reading for a person in normal health, which may depend to some extent on how his rule is orientated. If the reading is 38cm., he will find that a person with poor vitality will give a reading below this, say at 36cm. or lower. If the reading were 35cm. his nerves would be in a pretty bad state. On the other hand a reading of 40cm. would probably indicate an inflammatory or actively toxic condition, as is produced by influenza or catarrh. In this case the administration of a correct remedy would bring the reading back to 38cm. It is desirable to keep one's rule in one place, always orientated in the same direction.

The best orientation of a rule is a somewhat debatable point. For work with a Lesourd tape, which is made in France and used like a rule, the recommended orientation is N–S. With an ordinary 100cm. wooden rule my preference would be for an E–W orientation, with the radiesthetist facing north or south. Often the layout of a room and the arrangement of the furniture in it will determine how a rule can be most conveniently placed, and it is for the radiesthetist to find out how this affects his readings. I do not think there should be any real trouble on this score. In my own case, as it happens, I ordinarily face south.

There is nothing more that we can do with our rule without adding to our equipment, and so we must now acquire samples of liquid adrenalin and acetylcholine. Liquid adrenalin can be used as a witness or sample of the sympathetic nervous system and acetylcholine as one representing the parasympathetic nervous system. As I have previously explained elsewhere, adrenalin is secreted at the nerve ends of the sympathetic nervous system and acetylcholine at those of the parasympathetic nervous system.

We can use these two samples, or witnesses, in a number of ways. I shall in future refer to them, as I have done in the past, as S and P respectively. If I put S (a small quantity of liquid adrenalin in a glass vial) at 100cm. on my rule with a human specimen at 0cm., I will obtain a pendulum balance point for the sympathetic nervous system near the centre of the rule. A reading of 49 or 50cm. would be a normal reading, but 47cm. would indicate some loss of vitality. Low readings of both S and P may be taken as meaning that the patient is not very fit. Readings of 47cm. for both S and P are not uncommon and indicate that treatment is required. Lower readings, such as 45cm. or below, may indicate shock. On the other hand one may obtain a reading below 50cm. for S and above 50cm. for P. This indicates that the patient is fighting some fairly acute infection. Any two readings where P is greater than S, when both readings are below 50cm., may be taken to indicate tension or stress, due in all probability to infection of some kind. A favourable remedy should restore both S and P to 49–50cm. In the exceptional case where S is greater than P, we must assume a high degree of nervous tension, possibly of an emotional nature.

It is necessary at this point to refer to what I have called my polarity readings. We already know that with the patient's specimen at 0cm., an R reading (i.e. one obtained with no other sample on or adjacent to the rule) will be found by pendulum at, say, 38cm. If we place a sample of S on a rubber block adjacent to the patient's specimen, we may get the same balance point. On the other hand we may get one of, say, 36cm. This indicates some loss in the patient's normal vitality. Supposing we replace S by P. The reading may be at 38cm., or it may also go down to 36cm. Here again, with both readings at 36cm., the patient will be lacking in tone. The condition will be similar to that where tests for the sympathetic and para-sympathetic nervous systems are both low. On the other hand the P reading may go well above that for S, and we may have a polarity designated as 38–36/55. The number 38 refers to the R reading, 36 to the S polarity reading and 55 to the P polarity reading. Such readings are clear and very definite evidence that the patient is suffering from the effects of an acute infection. An attack of influenza could account for readings of this kind. Most organs might be affected and one would expect some considerable degree of toxicity. Homoeopathic potencies of 30c may be needed. Any remedy that will reduce such a P polarity reading to 10cm. or below is well indicated, and this in fact is an exceedingly useful test for appropriate remedies, particularly when the condition of the patient is so disorganised that accurate diagnosis is difficult, if not impossible. Generally speaking, whatever the polarity readings are in a particular case, any remedy which reduces the P polarity reading to below 10cm. is very well indicated. In the polarity given above, the R reading at 38cm. is normal, although the S and P readings are 'split' (i.e. they are *different*). A robust individual might give these readings, but more probably the *R* reading would be reduced, probably to 36cm., the same as for *S*. Where *S* and *P* both give the same readings but are below *R*, this indicates very definite nervous depletion. On the other hand readings in which *S* and *P* are the same, but above *R*, can be produced by over-stimulation through drugs or radionic treatment. If *S* and *P* are below *R* with a corresponding depleted nervous system, it may be better to check a remedy by finding to what extent it will increase the vitality reading of *R*. Where *S* and *P* polarity readings are both below *R*, while a good remedy tested on *P* will probably produce a reading at or below 10cm., it should also produce a reading of, say, 38cm., this being the normal *P* polarity reading. As long as the pendulist is clear in his own mind what he is testing, there should be no difficulty. Sometimes in a difficult case quite inexplicable readings are found, so much so that one can wonder what is happening.

The radiations of a patient whose system is badly disorganised may give readings which make little sense. Acute nervous depletion may upset all readings to such an extent that they are of little use from the diagnostic point of view. Every organ appears to be severely depleted. Once the system has been toned up, the position becomes clearer. A remedy which reduces the *P* polarity reading to below 10cm. will generally increase the *S* polarity reading, as also the *R* reading. An advantage of the radiesthetic method is that there are always ways in which a problem can be tackled. As treatment develops, the basic factors involved in a case gradually reveal themselves.

Chapter 4

Samples and Witnesses

We have seen how we can test the sympathetic and parasympathetic nervous systems with samples of liquid adrenalin and acetylcholine. We can in a similar way test other factors contributing to the health of an individual by means of samples. The late Dr. W. Guyon Richards used as samples urea and uric acid to determine the toxic condition of a patient. As his powers of mental dowsing developed (of which more anon), he came to use samples or witnesses less and less. But he never dispensed with samples of urea and uric acid.

The importance of urea was made very clear in one of the B.B.C. television presentations in the 'Your Life in Their Hands' series, in which a woman's kidneys had ceased to function during a pregnancy and an 'artificial kidney' was hastily substituted to deal with the accumulating toxins. As the patient's system was detoxicated, constant readings were taken of the level of urea in the blood. From a sample of urea in a small glass vial, we can get a very good idea of the state of a patient and whether he is suffering from infection.

If you place the sample at 100cm. on the rule with the saliva specimen at 0cm., you may obtain a balance point at 50cm. With many radiesthetists I believe this is regarded as the normal balance point, i.e. that indicated in a person in good health. However, in my own case the normal balance point for all *disease* conditions is 45cm. This I have confirmed over the years and it may be due to the fact that I am left-handed. As this book is based on my own experience, I will assume the 45cm. reading as the normal for all disease conditions. Thus, if we get a reading of 55cm., there is definite infection present. A uric acid sample is also very useful, and in most cases the readings for urea and uric acid will be the same. A reading for uric acid higher than urea indicates an acid condition, and one in particular in which the liver may need attention. I consider that Lycopodium is one of the best remedies, and probably the best, for dealing with this condition as such. If urea is higher than uric acid, Guyon Richards considered that this indicated the presence of virus infection. In analysing a case by radiesthetic methods, I think urea should always be tested, uric acid being only second in importance to it as a factor to test. When employing solid samples, I use urea and uric acid in 1x potency, but ordinary powdered samples of urea and uric acid should do just as well. In latter years I have used waveforms as produced by a radionic instrument instead, and for this I worked out my own rate for uric acid as 0·41. Actually this is not a disease rate, but I found it worked very well. We will be considering radionic instruments later.

We can use animal organs preserved in alcohol as samples. What are more convenient are specially prepared samples made in France representing the various bodily organs. These are known as witnesses, the best known in Britain being Turenne witnesses, after a French engineer of that name, who was also a highly competent radiesthetist. These witnesses are supplied in boxes of forty and comprise starch-impregnated powder in small glass vials. Turenne witnesses representing the various diseases to which man is prone are similarly available in boxes of forty.

These witnesses enable us to determine quickly the state of an organ. Supposing that we want to find out the condition of the liver of a patient, we place his specimen at 0cm. on the rule and the witness of liver at 100cm. We then find the balance point in just the same way as we would when testing for urea or uric acid. But in this case we are not testing a disease condition and the normal balance point is 50cm. If the patient's liver is normal, it should balance at 49–50cm. Personally, in making tests of this kind, I have always placed alongside the witness on a rubber block a sample of S (liquid adrenalin), as I am of the impression that this helps to stabilise the rule radiesthetically and makes it that much easier to obtain an accurate result. But it is by no means essential and seldom used, as far as I know, by other radiesthetists. A badly affected liver might be expected to give a reading of 45cm., but a reading of 47cm. or under suggests that the liver requires treatment. If the liver is highly toxic, i.e. if it is affected by some active bacterial or virus infection, or both, it is possible that a reading of 50–52cm. will be obtained. But in that case, if we put a sample of P (acetylcholine) alongside the witness, in all probability a reading well above 50cm. will result. A good remedy will very much reduce the reading for liver as tested on P. In all cases where the readings for an organ are higher when tested for P than they are for S, we can conclude that the organ is resisting some active infection. If the readings for an organ as tested on S and P are both the same, but materially lower than 50cm. (say 45cm.), we might say that the organ is in a shocked condition. They reveal a serious lack of function. Incidentally these readings have nothing to do with the polarity readings. If we want to find a remedy to deal with an infection, with the witness of the infection at 100cm. and the patient's specimen at 0cm., we place the remedy alongside the patient's specimen, just off the rule. If it is a good remedy the reading will be brought down from, say, 55cm. to 10cm., or lower. If we are using homoeopathic remedies, we will choose that potency which reduces the reading to the maximum extent. Possibly we may find it difficult to decide whether a remedy suits the condition best in a 6 or a 30 potency. In that case we can find which potency will give the highest reading when tested on the R reading, i.e. by finding to what extent this reading (obtained with nothing but the patient's specimen on the rule) is increased.

If the R reading is 38cm., a 6c potency may produce a reading of 70cm. and the 30c potency one of 80cm. In that case the 30c potency is the best potency. If the remedy is a good one for the case treated, it should be possible to find a balance point at near the 100cm. mark, with say 98cm. for the 30c potency and 95cm. for the 6c. Potencies can equally be tested on the P polarity. It is important to realise that in most rule tests one can obtain more than one balance point, so that it is necessary to have clearly in mind what one is looking for. As the operator progresses in his radiesthetic studies, he will modify his methods in the light of experience, perhaps substituting one balance point for another.

The Turenne list of the forty most common disease witnesses is as follows:

TABLE I

Syphilis	Enteritis
Gonococcus	Dysentery
Soft chancre	Typhoid
Pre-cancers	Paratyphoid A
Sarcoma	Paratyphoid B
Carcinoma	Scarlatina
Fibroma	Smallpox
Uterine fibroma	Chicken pox
Ovarian cyst	Measles
Tuberculosis	Cold
Pneumococcus	Influenza
T.B. Koch	Whooping cough
Staphylococcus aureus	Gout
Streptococcus	Rheumatism
Meningitis	Endocarditis
Encephalitis	Uric acid
Poliomyelitis	Poisons
Diptheria	Staphylococcus
Malaria	B. coli
Appendicitis	Internal parasites

Other Turenne witnesses of rarer diseases are also available. For instance, there are a number of witnesses of the different types of parasites and of tropical diseases.

Homoeopathic nosodes can also be employed for diagnosing disease conditions. These nosodes are potencies of specially prepared cultures and are useful when testing for a bacterium or virus which is not represented by the available witnesses. A list of forty nosodes covering disease conditions often found in practice are given below:

TABLE II

Bacillinum	Mucobacter
Tuberculinum	B. Influenzae
T.B. Bovinum	Bronchisepticus
Syphilinum	Influenza virus A
Gonococcus	Influenza virus B
Vaccinium	Influenza Asian
Sycosis	Aseptic meningitis
Carcinosin	Meningitis
B. coli	Encephalitis
Streptococcus	Poliomyelitis
Staphylococcus	Diptheria
Typhoidinum	Morbillinum
Paratyphoid	Rubella
Welchii	Varicella
Botulinum	Parotidinum
B. Gaertner	Pertussis
Faecalis	Pneumococcus
B. Morgan	Malaria
Dysentry	Anthrax
Septicaemia	Tetanus

Other nosodes which may also be useful for diagnostic and treatment purposes are:

TABLE III

B. Typhosus coli	Rabies (hydrophobia)
Bacillinum testis	Rous sarcoma
Corynebacterium coryzae	Scarlatina
Cancer serum	Scirrhinum
Enterococcus	Streptococcus agalactiae
Herpes simplex	Streptococcus haemolyticus
Herpes zoster	Streptococcus pyogenes
B. Hodgkini	Streptococcus rheumaticus
Influenza Spanish	Streptococcus viridans

B. Koch–Weeks	Staphylococcus aureus
Lueticum	Staphylococcus abdominalis
Medorrhinum	Staphylococcus pyogenes
Micrococcus catarrhalis	T.B. Avian
Morgan-Gaertner	T.B. Denys
Mutabilis	T.B. Koch
Morax-Axenfeldt	T.B. Marmorek
Pestis	T.B. meningitis
Psorinum	Tinea pedis
Proteus	Variolinum

There are several ways in which nosodes can be employed for testing for infection. The simplest would be to find what effect they had on the R rule reading. Place the nosode alongside the patient's specimen at 0cm. and find to what extent the reading is increased. The nosode, or nosodes, which give the highest readings would certainly suggest that the patient was infected by the appertaining bacteria, viruses, or their toxins. This question of toxins is important. Often enough, in tests of this kind, it is the toxins of the disease rather than the disease itself, as represented by living organisms, which produce the readings indicating infection. For instance, the toxins of influenza, which are highly poisonous, may remain in the system of a patient long after he has succumbed to an epidemic attack of influenza. Until these toxins are eliminated the patient cannot make a full recovery.

Another method is to see what effect a nosode will have on the reading for urea. Supposing that this reading is 60cm., indicating a fairly high degree of infection. A nosode placed in radiative contact with, i.e. alongside, the patient's specimen at 0cm., but just off the rule, will reduce this reading considerably if the disease it represents is active in the patient's system. If several 30c nosodes are tested, one or two will probably reduce the readings most, to perhaps 10cm. or less. In all such tests the results depend on the activation of the disease, i.e. to what extent the affecting organisms are active in the patient. Toxins latent in the system of the patient may also be activated by the subsequent invasion of some new virus or bacterium. This is a common experience in radiesthetic work. Some old malarial toxins will often 'boil up' in the system during an attack of influenza and a reaction for malaria will be obtained. These toxins need to be treated equally with the invading pathogenic organism.

It should be remembered that a 30c nosode represents a fairly high degree of activity and in a very mild attack of influenza virus A, for example, one might expect a 6c nosode to produce a somewhat lower reading when tested on urea than a 30c nosode would. While

6c nosodes of some diseases are available, they are seldom, if ever, employed in treatment and most radiesthetists would be content to have in their possession a set of 30c nosodes only. A 6c nosode represents only a very mild infection.

Another way in which these nosodes can be used for diagnostic purposes is to place the nosode at 100cm. with the patient's specimen at 0cm. and a sample of *S* (liquid adrenalin) in radiesthetic contact with the nosode. Then move the pendulum slowly up the rule from 0cm. until a balance point is found. This may be, say, 10, 15, 20 or 25 cm. A reading of 10cm. would probably indicate the presence of the corresponding disease active in the patient, whereas a reading of over 15 or 20cm. should be taken as negative. In assessing the position in any one case, one would naturally take into account the comparative readings of all nosodes tested. One reading lower than the rest would be a significant indication of the presence of an active infection represented by the nosode producing that reading.

Supposing the reading is 10cm. If we want to find whether a particular remedy will deal with this infection, place it alongside the specimen at 0cm. and find to what extent the reading is increased from 10cm. If the new balance point goes up to 40cm. or above, it is very well indicated.

Supposing that a particular organ is giving a bad reading and it is desired to find what infection is responsible for it. If it is the stomach and it gives a reading on the rule of 45cm., a nosode representing the responsible infection placed alongside the specimen should return the reading to 50cm. Another method would be to place a sample of *P* (acetylcholine) alongside the stomach witness at 100cm. and find to what extent the nosode will reduce the reading on the rule.

While the experienced practitioner will decide on his own methods of test, it is a good plan for the novice in radiesthesia to study all methods and try them out. He will in this way become familiar with work on the rule and increase his skill thereby. Other methods of employing Turenne witnesses and nosodes can be used in conjunction with 'The Triangle' and with radionic instruments. These are dealt with in subsequent chapters.

Chapter 5

The Triangle

In the rule method already described one measures distances. In the triangle method one measures angles. Some medical radiesthetists work with triangles, others with rules, and still others with both. I prefer to regard the two methods as complementary. One can check a result obtained by one method with tests by the second method.

Just as there are many ways of working with a pendulum on a rule, so different practitioners will work somewhat differently with a triangle. I believe Mrs. Gladys Barraclough was the first radiesthetist in Britain to develop a technique of working on a triangle to a high degree of precision, and it was through her advice and assistance that other radiesthetists found their way to working with a triangle.

It was through knowing Dr. Guyon Richards that I myself came to use a rule, and it was much more recently that I have put the triangle to everyday practical use. Each method has its own advantages and can give clearer indications according to the particular type of test.

My own method of using the triangle is quite simple and I shall restrict myself to it. First I should say that it is important to draw out the diagram to the correct scale. The diameter of the surrounding circle of the diagram I use is 25cm. and the contained triangle is equilateral. The details of the diagram will be seen from the accompanying illustration. Being left-handed, I find it convenient to place the patient's specimen at A and witnesses of what it is desired to test at B. It may well be that right-handed operators may prefer to place the specimen and witness the other way round. It is simply a matter of convenience and finding what arrangement suits the individual best.

Supposing that you want to find whether a patient has a streptococcal infection. With the saliva specimen at A and the streptococcal witness at B (or vice versa), you hold the pendulum by its thread over the centre of the circle. You will find that it oscillates generally in a direction somewhere to the right of D. It may give a reading of 10° or it may give one of 60°. The greater the angle the pendulum makes with the line CD, the more positive the indication is of the

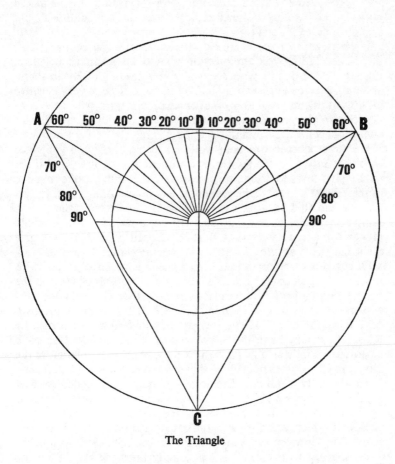

The Triangle

microbe or its toxin being actively present in the patient. A reading of 90° would represent an acute infection and the pendulum will seldom go beyond this point.

With the patient's specimen at A and nothing at B, the pendulum will balance somewhere between 0° and 30°. If the patient holds an appropriate remedy in his hand and, remembering that he is linked radiesthetically to his specimen at A, the operator's pendulum should swing round to 0°, or D.

If we assume a particular case where the patient's reading is 20°, the same reading for an infection should be taken as negative. Probably most disease witnesses will give a reading of 20° or thereabouts. Any reading such as 50° or more will be a very positive indication. Quite probably one or two witnesses will give considerably higher readings than the rest. These will be the disease conditions which the practitioner should treat.

If a streptococcal witness provides a reading of 60° and you place with it at B (just inside the circle) a witness of, say, liver, and if the reading increases to 65cm., we can assume that the microbe is active in the patient's liver. If the reading is less than 60°, it is not. In this way we can find to what extent an organ is infected. Our disease sample may consist of a Turenne witness, a nosode, or a specially prepared bacterial culture. A nosode, though potentised, will give the same result on the triangle as a Turenne witness.

Our next problem is to find what remedy is required to deal with the offending microbe. Let us take again a reading of 60° for the streptococcal infection. If we place a remedy that will deal effectively with the bacterium just outside the circle at B, the pendulum will beat along the line CD. The remedy may be Sulphur or it may be Rhus tox. It may be in the 6c potency or it may be 30c. Because a 6c potency is indicated as the correct remedy by an oscillation in the direction CD, it does not follow that a 30c potency will do the same. More generally it will not. The potencies most often needed are 6 or 12, according to which of these two potencies are usually employed by the practitioner. But this does not mean that 3x potencies cannot be found which are also well indicated, assuming that it is considered that low potencies are wanted to deal with the infection.

Testing organs is carried out in exactly the same way. With the patient's specimen at A and an organ witness of, say, stomach at B, the pendulum will give a reading of between 0° and 10° if the organ is in pretty good shape. A reading of 30° or more should be taken as showing a fair degree of imbalance. A suitable remedy placed against the organ witness at B (just outside the circle) will return the pendulum to 0°.

It is important that a prescribed remedy should not only correct a specific imbalance, but that it should also be as far as possible constitutional to the patient at the time of test. Often enough the choice has to be made between two or more remedies and the practitioner has to decide which is best for his patient. If we place a remedy at B with the patient's specimen at A, the pendulum may give a reading such as 50°, 70° or 90°. Generally speaking, the greater the angle the better suited the remedy is. What we are measuring in effect is, as I believe, a deficiency. Only a remedy whose vibration is in some sense deficient can be safely repeated in the form of a prescription.

We already know several methods by which remedies can be chosen according to their general suitability as determined on a rule, the most simple of which is finding what remedy will increase the vitality or R reading (about 38cm.) to the greatest extent. Working on the triangle, if we place a witness of sympathetic nervous system (S) at B, a suitable remedy should restore any imbalance in the reading to 0°. This is a very good general test. Another method which I have tried out is to place the remedy at B which, as we already know, will give a fairly high reading such as 70°, 80° or even 90° if it is well indicated. However, if we place first a sample of S and then of P at C, the pendulum should oscillate along CD if the remedy is precisely tuned to the patient. By finding an acceptable remedy in this way, we are in fact equating the energy of the remedy to that required by the patient. If a patient is tested in this way soon after he has taken a homoeopathic dose, it may be difficult or impossible to find a remedy which is suitable for him at the moment of test. Anything he takes further at this time would in all probability constitute an overdose, i.e. an over-stimulation. On the other hand, if a patient is already over-stimulated, it should be possible by this method to find a remedy which would antidote what has been previously taken. In other words, it would lower the energy content of the patient to his normal level. To put the matter as clearly as possible, a remedy which is well indicated when tested, shall we say, on the sympathetic nervous system, would be contra-indicated immediately after a dose of that remedy has been taken by the patient. In homoeopathic treatment we are dealing with energy levels both in the remedies and within the patient himself. It is next to impossible to carry this out accurately without some method of radiesthetic testing. It is this energy level produced in the homoeopathic remedy through potentisation which gives it its great curative power.

With two remedies separately tested at B and each giving a reading of 80°, if they go well together and are tested together at B (just inside the circle), we might expect the reading to go to 90°. If they are unsuited, a reading of something less than 80° will be obtained.

The rule can equally be employed for testing for compatibility. Supposing we have chosen two remedies as being suitable for treating a disease condition, the reading for urea being 70cm. Each remedy tested separately may reduce this reading to 10cm. But together they may take the reading down to 5cm. On the other hand they may send it up to 15 or 20cm., this being a clear indication that the remedies are incompatible. In taking the pendulum down the rule in a test of this kind, no resistance may be felt right down to the patient's specimen. The remedies are then compatible and very well indicated.

It may sometimes surprise the beginner to find how very definitely the pendulum will decide the correct balance point. If it is moved, however slightly, up or down the rule, the operator may feel quite a strong resistance against it going further. Instead of a rule, Dr. Richards used the 48in. edge of his table and he found his balance point by gyrations instead of oscillations. At the same time I think a more accurate balance point can be found by making the pendulum oscillate across a rule. It is all a matter of what method suits the individual best. Sooner or later the radiesthetist will find his own special methods of testing, which he will modify as his experience grows.

The triangle is very useful for quick and accurate determination of the state of the endocrine glands. It is not unusual to obtain a reading of 40° or more for a badly balanced gland. Any unfit person feeling 'under the weather' will show some imbalance in his endocrine system, and he will feel much better the moment it returns to normal function. It is important therefore in a prescription to make sure that the endocrines are suitably treated, together with other imbalances. Often enough, testing out a remedy on a badly functioning endocrine is a useful way of assessing its general suitability.

When the endocrine system is seriously at fault, it will generally be found that the vitamins show deficiency. Vitamin and endocrine function appear to be closely connected, and a course of vitamins is often useful for helping to restore the endocrine system to normal activity. We often talk about vitamin deficiencies. These indeed occur. At the same time, with a person living on a well-balanced diet, it may be more a question of vitamin activity being depressed by some infection or toxin rather than one of actual deficiency. In either case a course of vitamins will help to restore balance.

Vitamins can, of course, be destroyed by toxins or some other cause, and often enough they will be needed in treatment for this reason. In a gross case of toxaemia Vitamin C may give a very low reading and I have sometimes obtained very low readings for Vitamin D where the bone condition has been affected. Alcohol tends to produce deficiencies in Vitamin B. Mineral deficiencies may need attention and Calcarea carb. is a remedy which is often needed to restore calcium balance. Here again it may be more a case of faulty calcium metabolism than actual calcium deficiency. We could not expect Calcarea carb. 6 to replace actual calcium deficiency by weight, but it will certainly help the patient to absorb calcium present in his diet. Only calcium in solid unpotentised form will actually replace a deficiency. But there is everything to be said for restoring this deficiency by providing a diet rich in calcium and ensuring its absorption through the administration of calcium in potency.

Endocrine glands can be tested with dried gland extracts, Turenne witnesses or potencies. I often use 6c potencies myself. The effect of potentising a product appears to make no difference to readings obtained by it on the triangle and the stronger radiesthetic influence of a potency should be an advantage.

I do not think specific vitamin treatment should be employed unless there is a clear case for it. Vitamin 'deficiencies' are often found to be corrected on test on the triangle by a remedy which is dealing with some overriding infection or toxin. This applies equally to the treatment of the endocrine glands. On the other hand, if a patient is very debilitated with acute endocrine and vitamin imbalances, a course of vitamins should help to restore his vitality when given in conjunction with whatever other treatment is indicated.

As I have previously stated, both the rule and the triangle methods can be employed together when testing a case. I have always found it necessary myself to stand when rule testing, whereas one can do triangle testing sitting down. To this extent the triangle has an advantage and may be used for this reason more often than it would otherwise be. It is important in all radiesthetic work that the operator should not get overtired. When travelling it is often impossible to find the facilities for rule testing, whereas a table can almost always be found for work on the triangle.

Chapter 6

Testing with Radionic Instruments

In *I.M.R.R.* I described how I used a radionic instrument for diagnostic purposes in conjunction with a rule. For the benefit of those who have not read the book, it is necessary to go over this ground briefly again. The instruments I have used are Delawarr instruments and either a diagnostic instrument or a broadcast instrument can equally well be employed. The main difference is that a diagnostic instrument takes up more room on the table and the dials lie horizontally, whereas the dials are arranged on a vertical panel on a broadcast instrument. A broadcast instrument is also cheaper to buy.

The arrangement I use myself is a 100cm. rule connected to a broadcast instrument by what I have described as a 'vial connection'. This instrument is designed solely for the purpose of treating patients by sending out to them through the ether specific radiations, the link between instrument and patient being provided by placing the patient's specimen on either one, or both, of the plates provided (where the instrument has more than one plate). Some of these instruments are made so that they can also be used for transmitting microsonic radiations direct to the patient, who sits in front of the instrument about 4ft. away. In this case the instrument is connected to a mains supply. But as already inferred, the instruments can be employed for diagnosis in connection with a rule.

The waveform of the organ or condition it is desired to test is produced in the instrument by setting the appropriate rate for the organ or condition on the dials and transferred to one end of the rule via the vial connection. This connection consists simply of two glass vials linked together by a thread, or piece of string, tied at each end to the neck of one of the vials. The arrangement is shown in the accompanying illustration. One vial is placed on the plate of the instrument and the other at 100cm. on the rule. Any slack in the thread is taken up by winding it up round the neck of one, or both, of the vials. It may strengthen the radiesthetic connection to introduce the ends of the thread to the inside of the vials. The vial at 100cm. then replaces solid samples or Turenne witnesses, and tests can be made for assessing the condition of organs and the presence of micro-organisms in the same way as with witnesses.

Each broadcast instrument has nine dials arranged in three horizontal tiers. Dial 1 is calibrated in 10's from 0 to 100, whereas the other eight dials are calibrated from 0 to 10. Dial 1 is used only to denote a disease condition. Thus, if we want to put up the rate for the common cold virus, which is 40652, we set dial 1 at 40, dial 2 (on the right of dial 1) at 6, dial 3 at 5 and dial 4 (the first dial in the second tier) at 2. On the other hand, if we want to set up the rate for an organ such as the heart, which is 5238, we leave dial 1 at 0 and set dial 2 at 5, dial 3 at 2, and so on. There are certain disease rates which have only two digits and these are set on dial 1. Thus 10 is the rate for deficiency, 40 for inflammation, 50 for cancer and 70 for pain. So that if we set up on our instrument the rate 405238, i.e. the rate for heart preceded on dial 1 by the rate for inflammation, we have a combined rate for 'inflammation of the heart'. Inflammation generally denotes toxaemia, and if we test a patient for inflammation of the heart and the result is positive, we can assume that the heart is to some extent toxic.

If a patient has a streptococcal infection, it may affect his heart in addition to other organs. We now know how to discover whether his heart is toxic, but we can make a more specific test to see if it is affected by the streptococcus. If the infection is Strep. pyogenes, we set the rate for this, 6057, on the instrument. This will give a positive reading. If we add to this rate that for the heart, we have the combined rate for 'streptococcal infection of the heart'. If the positive reading previously found is increased, we know that the heart is being poisoned, to whatever extent, by the streptococcus. If the reading is actually less, we can conclude that the heart is not being appreciably affected by it.

We must now see how we actually take our measurements. Let us assume that the rate for heart is set on the instrument and this is connected to the 100cm. mark on the rule by means of the vial connection. The patient's specimen is placed at 0cm. and, of course, dial 1 will be set at 0, as we are not diagnosing a disease condition. As with solid samples it is my practice to place a sample of S on a rubber block alongside the rule at 100cm., but this is by no means essential.

If we now gently oscillate the pendulum near the 50cm. mark, we will probably find that it balances at 49–50cm. which denotes normal function. If it balances at 45cm., function of the heart is badly affected. If we now set dial 1 at 40, we may find the pendulum balances at 45cm. which, as previously explained, is my neutral balance point for all disease conditions. In that case the heart is non-toxic. If the balance point is 50cm. or higher, the heart is definitely toxic. We can now set dial 1 at 10, denoting deficiency of the heart. If the pendulum balance point is still 45cm., there is no deficiency in heart function. But if the reading goes up to 50cm. or more, there is lack of function. Sometimes this test gives a better indication for heart function than when using the rate for heart only, especially if there is toxaemia present. Nevertheless, a heart which is badly lacking in function, more particularly perhaps when actual heart disease is present, may give a reading such as 46 cm., with dial 1 at 0.

By using the rates 50 and 70 on dial 1, we can test for cancer of the heart (a hypothetical condition) and pain in the heart (much more probable). The remedy for such conditions can be found in exactly the same way as when we are using solid samples. If a streptococcal infection is responsible for the abnormal heart condition, an appropriate remedy for dealing with the streptococcus placed in radiative contact with the saliva specimen (or blood spot, if that is what we are using) will reduce the readings for 'inflammation of heart' etc. to 10cm. or below. In all these tests dial 9 in the bottom right-hand corner, which is known as the 'measuring dial', is set at 8. When using a diagnostic instrument by the 'stick' method, which is the prescribed method as laid down in radionic practice, dial 9 measures the degree of function or activity in an organ or disease condition. The setting on dial 9 for normal function of an organ is 8 and, as in the rule method we are determining activity and function through our readings on the rule, this dial should remain at 8 throughout our tests.

In these tests with a rule and radionic instrument, the instrument need not be connected to earth, as is the case when broadcast treatment is being given. Also the vials should be of a suitable size. When I first discovered the vial connection method, I found that the vials should be of a size not smaller than ½oz. In fact ½oz. vials are probably as good as any, especially those 7cm. high (including the neck) by 2 cm. diameter. These vials act as resonance chambers and are not effective as such unless they are of a suitable size.

We are not concerned in this book with standard radionic practice, which can be studied in other publications and was briefly described in *I.M.R.R.* The pendulum is the most sensitive radiesthetic detector that we have and is the one on which I have depended for all my radiesthetic work.

When using the rule-cum-radionic instrument method, nosodes are often valuable for diagnosing the condition of an organ. Supposing that the stomach is badly affected, giving a reading for 'inflammation of the stomach' of 65cm. If we place 30c. nosodes in turn alongside the specimen at 0 cm., we will probably find that one or more nosodes produce a reading of 10cm. or less. We can then conclude that the virus, microbe or disease condition denoted by these nosodes is affecting the stomach, and this will be a useful guide to treatment. It also avoids the necessity of setting up the rates for each of the organisms tested.

We can also use the nosodes in a different way. Supposing that 'inflammation of the stomach' gives a reading of 65cm. as before. If we place the nosodes in turn alongside the 100cm. mark instead of at 0cm., we will find that the nosodes representing organisms which are active in the organ give a higher reading on the scale than the others. In practice this test can only be made usefully when the rate set on the instrument gives its own reading of, say, not more than 55cm., as there must be room on the scale above that figure for higher differentiated readings.

Where the method may have a definite use is in the determination of toxins. Supposing we put up the rate for Streptococcus and obtain a reading of 55–60cm. If we place a sample of Septicaemin 30 alongside the 100cm. mark and the reading goes up to 70–75cm., we can infer that the patient is being affected more by the toxins of the disease than by the disease itself. On the other hand, if the reading remains at 55–60cm., or is even reduced, I would assume that I was dealing with the active pathogen at that stage rather than with its toxins. After an attack of influenza, influenza toxins may remain in the system a long time unless steps are taken to eliminate them. This applies equally to other infections. Occasionally when testing a case, the general rate for toxins will be positive while those for viruses, bacteria and poisons are negative. We can then find which nosodes increase the general rate reading for toxins by placing each in turn opposite the 100cm. mark. We could, of course, equally well test for specific toxins by placing the nosodes alongside the specimen at 0cm. and finding which reduce the readings to 10cm. or below. The Delawarr Laboratories provide rates for specific toxins and in obscure or subacute cases these rates can be especially useful. In a miasmatic case with a T.B. diathesis, the rate for T.B. toxins may be positive while other tests for tuberculosis are negative. Many people suffer to some extent from hereditary toxins, and these may show up strongly in radiesthetic tests during an illness to which the patient is subject. Although in this country tuberculosis is a dying disease, T.B. toxins are often found in patients due to its virulence in past generations. Such patients may all the more easily contract a new T.B. infection unless the toxins are eliminated. Reactions for syphilis, gonorrhoea, measles and whooping-cough are often obtained in patients where the origins of the disease go back many years. The homoeopathic remedy, perhaps allied to radionic broadcast treatment, is a potent means of eliminating such toxins from the system.

Not only can we make pendulum tests by the instrument and rule method, but equally we can use the instrument in combination with the triangle. The instrument is connected to the triangle with the vial connection by placing one vial on the plate of the instrument and the other at B, just inside the circle. In this case all we need to do in testing an organ is to set up its rate on the instrument and take the pendulum reading. A healthy organ will balance at 0°–10°, but if it is toxic the reading will be increased to 30° or more. Suitable remedies will be found, as with solid samples, by placing them in turn close to the vial, but just outside the circle. When using the triangle I doubt if there is ever any advantage in using the rates for 'inflammation' or 'deficiency'. One tests the rate for an organ or disease condition in exactly the same way as if one was using solid (or liquid) samples. One is simply measuring an imbalance. The higher the angle reading, the greater the imbalance shown by the organ, and the more acute the disease condition is. Working with both a rule and a triangle, I have seldom used the instrument-cum-triangle arrangement as I find it rather clumsy. It can be useful on occasion for making a double check.

Occasionally, when testing an organ, the pendulum will oscillate to the left of CD. This can be taken as indicating an active but highly toxic organ. If the reading is 10° measured to the left of D, we can call this a positive reading of +10°. The organ is over-active, over-stimulated by toxins. In most tests on the triangle readings for organs are negative, those of 20° or more very definitely needing attention.

Chapter 7

The Psychic Factor

Before we proceed to discuss case-taking, it is necessary to say something about the psychic factor in dowsing. By psychic we are referring to a department of mental activity involving extra-sensory perception, often referred to as E.S.P. Some dowsers have a very definite psychic gift, or ability. They can, for instance, ask questions and obtain answers by pendulum reaction. If you need an answer badly and it is important that you should have one, you may be able to get the right answer through your pendulum. Generally questions are put to the pendulum so that the answer is YES or NO. Thus it is that you might be very well able to find out whether a friend has gone away and, if so, where.

This sort of extra-sensory perception is often seen in animals. Dogs have been known to get wildly excited when their master was about to arrive home at a time when no one was expecting him. In human beings the pendulum is often useful as a means of bringing this extra-sensory perception into action. It may be a means of interpreting to the conscious mind knowledge which is already apprehended in the subconscious. There have, of course, been many instances of people involuntarily exercising this gift without a pendulum. It is not very unusual for a person to know instinctively when a friend, perhaps living far away in a distant part of the world, is very ill, or dying.

We may take it as a fact that everyone has some degree of E.S.P. and that it is often in action, whether we appreciate it or not. People quite often have a strong hunch about something with no apparent reason, which turns out to be justified. It is a not uncommon experience for a medical radiesthetist, when diagnosing a case, to find that although he had been inadvertently using the wrong human specimen, the answers he obtains broadly relate to the patient he is thinking about.

Some radiesthetists can obtain a great deal of information about a patient by the psychic method, where others would use witnesses. For instance, it is possible with the help of a diagram and a pendulum and the specimen of the patient under consideration to find out what infections he is suffering from, simply by saying out loud each infection in turn and noting the reaction of the pendulum on the diagram. Another method for the operator is to run the forefinger of the free hand down a list of infections and, while keeping the patient well in mind, leave the pendulum to indicate which infection, or infections, the patient has in his system. The results may be more satisfactory if the patient's specimen is brought into radiative contact in some way or other with the operator. One way would be for him to hold the specimen against the thread of the pendulum in his pendulum hand. If the patient is present, he could place his right hand on the right shoulder of the operator.

There is one important point to be remembered where E.S.P. comes into play. The more the operator knows about the person or the situation concerned, the more accurate should be the results. A man becomes aware intuitively of the death of a friend. We can be sure this would not have happened if he had not known him well. By knowing him he has become attuned to his wavelength, as it were. He is in telepathic *rapport*.

The most fascinating aspect of the psychic method for the dowser is undoubtedly map-dowsing. A dowser can go over some ground with his rod or pendulum and detect underground streams, faults and fissures. The explanation usually given for this is that he is detecting some influence or radiation emanating from the underground source through neuro-muscular reaction. It has been suggested that any such influence is associated with the action of cosmic rays. What we do know is that the air over an underground stream or fault becomes ionised. There is some actual physical disturbance.

The interesting point is that a dowser can equally well detect underground streams, faults and fissures from a map. If he goes over the map exactly as he would go over the actual ground, he should get exactly the same reactions, provided the map is drawn to a suitable scale. It does not seem to matter very much whether the map is printed, or whether it comprises only a rough sketch. But the probability is that the results will be more dependable if the information given on the map does present a fairly accurate idea of what the local features are. Here surely we have a most interesting example of E.S.P., all the more interesting by the fact that map-dowsing is commonly employed by field dowsers as part of their professional work. If their work was not dependable, their employers would soon have little use for them.

On the Continent there has in the past been a sharp division between those who believed that all dowsing was essentially of a psychic, or mental, nature and those who believed that it was physical. There is a similar, if largely unexpressed, cleavage in Britain today. It is not unusual to hear a radiesthetist say that all dowsing is purely 'mental' and that any value that witnesses, for instance, have is only subjective. At the same time I find it very difficult to believe that precise radiesthetic measurements taken on a rule or diagram with the help of witnesses could be equally well taken without witnesses. When one measures, say, the functional activity of the liver of a patient with his specimen at 0cm. on a rule and a liver witness at 100cm. and obtains a reading of, shall we say, 47cm., I can only believe that one is locating a balance point between the radiesthetic influence of the liver witness and that of the liver of the patient as represented in his specimen. In making a diagnosis with witnesses, one may have to make fifty or more individual tests. If the accuracy of the results depends entirely on the psychic ability of the operator, his psychic gifts must be of a high order indeed!

Towards the end of his life the late Dr. Guyon Richards came to rely almost entirely on his psychic ability and obtained readings on his rule (in his case the 48in. edge of his table) purely by mental concentration. But I am sure that the readings he obtained were only very loosely related to the actual intensity of what he was measuring.

I remember how a friend of mine, who consulted him on my recommendation, told me that he had obtained a reading for her heart of 0cm. I told her that she had no right to be alive! In checking endocrine glands his pendulum not infrequently ran down the scale from the 24in. mid-point of the table to 4in., i.e. to ⅙ of normal activity. I believe such readings were simply a convention personal to Dr. Richards and which he was fully able to interpret to his own satisfaction. There was no question of getting an accurate balance point on a rule. To him, I am sure, they simply meant that such endocrines, or whatever he was testing, were deficient in their action to a very considerable degree—that and nothing more.

He actually obtained his readings by pendulum gyrations and not oscillations, which is perhaps not the best way to get a precise balance point. In obtaining readings of 4in., his hand would go straight down the rule without a moment's hesitation and gyrate at that figure. He seemed to know instinctively, or by 'feel', the condition he was testing. In determining what pathogenic organisms were actively present in his patient, he would get him to place his left hand at the left-hand corner of the table with the palm pointing towards the centre, or put his specimen there, and he would rotate his pendulum a few inches to the right of the mid-point. He would first ask how many organisms there were, counting one, two, three, etc. When he came to the right number, the pendulum would stop with a jerk. He would then run over the various infections by name, the pendulum reacting in exactly the same way when he came to one which was present in the patient. It is significant, however, that he always checked his prescription with actual samples of urea and uric acid, and with actual drugs.

Dr. Richards was, of course, a past master in the art of medical radiesthesia and had previously done a vast amount of very precise research work on lines somewhat similar to those used by Dr. Albert Abrams. He published many of his results in *The Chain of Life*. He once told me he could not have done the sort of pendulum work he did without his previous very extensive experience, which involved close tuning with rheostats and reactions by means of percussion on the abdominal wall of his subject—in his case his secretary, Mr. Smith.

We find the psychic method employed very obviously in the orthodox method of making a diagnosis with a radionic diagnostic instrument. The patient's specimen is placed in one of the wells at the top of the right-hand panel and the rate for the disease condition which it is desired to treat set up on the dials. To find the cause, or causes, of the disease, the Cause Sheets are placed in turn on the left-hand panel and the cursor moved slowly down from the top of the sheet to the bottom. At the same time the operator is stroking the rubber pad with the fingers of the right hand and asking himself, as the cursor passes over each printed line, whether what that line represents is a factor contributing to the disease condition. If it is, he immediately obtains a stick, i.e. the rubber feels rough and sticky to his fingers and produces a characteristic crisp noise known as a 'stick'.

Some operators are extremely competent in working these diagnostic instruments, but it must be understood that if for a moment their attention is distracted in any way, they may miss a vital clue to the correct diagnosis of their patient. I believe that comparatively few people have the faculty of using these instruments in this way to the pitch of perfection required to ensure a satisfactory analysis. This is one reason why I devised an alternative method of using these instruments in conjunction with a rule and a pendulum, where each condition it is desired to test is set up on the dials. This can, of course, take a great deal of time, but one learns to know what rates it is really necessary to test in a particular case. The setting up of rates can also be avoided to some extent by using nosodes in conjunction with the rule, with or without a radionic instrument, and as a further power to our elbow we can use a rule or triangle with witnesses.

The reader should by now have a better idea of what we mean by psychic dowsing or, as many people prefer it, mental dowsing. By way of explanation we might say that in operating an instrument by the conventional method, the operator watches each condition on the Cause Sheet (or whatever other sheet is being used) that may contribute to the disease condition of the patient as it passes under the cursor and creates in his brain the waveform of the condition. When this condition on the Cause Sheet is a factor contributing to the disease condition in the patient as set on the dials, there is syntonisation between the waveform of the condition of the patient, i.e. that produced inside the resonance chamber of the instrument as determined by the setting of the dials, and that created in the brain of the operator, resonance between patient and operator thus being produced, signified by a stick. The power of the operator to tune his thoughts in to whatever cause, disease or organ is printed on the sheet he is using so as to produce a stick when this condition, whatever it is, is contributing to the disease state of the patient as represented by the rate set on the dials and its corresponding waveform inside the resonance chamber (which is itself tuned to the patient's specimen), is a faculty which must vary widely between individuals.

It has to be admitted that, despite all that has been written, we still know very little about the nature of radiesthesia. But we do know some very remarkable things about it. We know, for instance, that there is some kind of link between a person and some physical attribute of his, be it a blood smear, saliva specimen, urine or hair. For once a practitioner has obtained such a specimen from a patient, any diagnosis which he makes of that patient afterwards with the help of that specimen refers to the condition of the patient *at the moment it is made*. That is indeed a remarkable fact, but were it not so, it would not be possible to broadcast treatment through space by means of a radionic instrument or a diagram (as is sometimes done), using the patient's specimen. I have myself had occasion to examine the condition of patients living abroad with specimens which were several years old.

The last thing I would wish to do would be to deny the claims of some radiesthetists as to what they are able to achieve at the psychic level, with or without instruments or witnesses. Some claim that they can get as good results with written samples (i.e. word-witnesses) as with actual physical witnesses. No doubt they can, depending on the type of test they are making. The word-witness helps the operator to concentrate his mind on a particular item and, so to speak, produce its waveform in his brain. It is more difficult to understand the claim that has often been made in radiesthetic literature on the Continent that a word-witness can be treated in such a way that it can become in very truth as much a physical witness of some particular item as a sample or witness of that item as ordinarily understood. However, that is something which cannot be discussed here.

Personally I place my stand on the belief that there is no real antagonism between the two schools of mental and physical dowsing. I am reminded of the radio parlour game 'Twenty Questions' where the question-master says that the object on the card has 'physical connections'. I believe that what is implicit in radiesthesia is a force, a medium in its own right, which is of a paraphysical nature and has connections with both Mind and Matter. I believe its connections with both are authentic and objective and follow natural laws, laws controlling the action of the paraphysical world, just as laws control the physical world.

In my own researches I have at times spent hours trying to obtain objective readings on a rule somewhat on the lines used by Bovis and Brunler, including the well-known 'brain readings'. Sometimes my results were encouraging, but too often they would not bear repetition. I came to the conclusion that my failures were due to there not being a proper physical basis for my experiments. On the other hand, when I was using samples or waveforms, it took me very little time to realise when my results were repetitive. That is the acid test. For accurate arithmetical results on a rule, I am convinced that they are dependent on there being a correct physical basis. It is perhaps significant that Bovis always claimed that his work was based on physical law, that he could interpret his results in Ångström units.

Reverting to myself, once I had the idea of using S and P for my polarity test, it took very little time to discover that it was repetitive and gave objective information about the state of a patient. At the time I discovered my vial connection, I first used ½oz. vials. Then I thought that for convenience I might use smaller vials, say 2-drachm. They simply did not work. They were too small to act efficiently as resonant chambers. If this method of testing with rates was only subjective, it would not, of course, have mattered what size the vials were.

Some people believe that the rates used in radionics have no physical basis, that it is only the belief in their authenticity that helps the operator to get the results he wants, whereas he could as easily get them without the rates. In support of this they claim that different operators use different rates to test the same item. It is true that different rates will produce waveforms which on test closely relate to the same item and which can be used satisfactorily in practice. So also will different witnesses representing different strains of influenza virus all give positive reactions in a case in which influenza is present. But this does not mean that either the rates or the witnesses are faulty—or should we say phoney?

Nothing has ever happened in my own limited experience of

Vial connection between Delawarr instrument and 100cm. mark on rule, with sample of *S* (liquid adrenalin) on rubber block

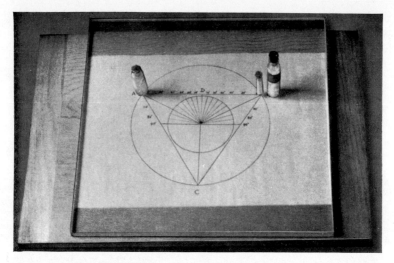

Arrangement on triangle for testing a patient's saliva specimen (on left) against a disease witness (on right). A suitable remedy, placed outside the circle (as shown), should make the pendulum oscillate up and down (along CD)

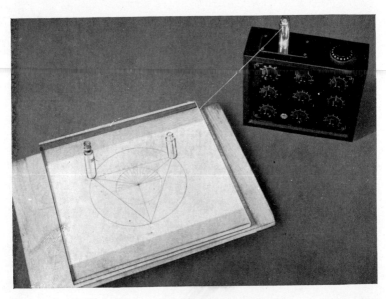

The specimen of a patient can be tested on the triangle in conjunction with the vial connection to instrument broadcast treatment, and indeed of direct microsonic treatment also, to suggest that the rates were unimportant. The evidence I have had has been all the other way, as will be shown later. Only too often results have been disappointing unless I found a rate that really mattered, one that was pin-pointing fundamental causes in the case. Nevertheless, when a patient's specimen is placed correctly on a radionic instrument and the instrument is properly tuned in, that patient will receive fundamental energy, whatever the rate that is set up. To that extent he may receive some benefit.

We have a long way to go in elucidating the science of radiesthesia. Researchers like Baron von Reichenbach, Max Freedom Long and Professor Tromp have made important contributions. More recently Dr. Aubrey Westlake has done notable service to the cause with his book, *The Pattern of Health*, especially in his emphasis on the connection between the dowsing faculty and the counterpart etheric bodies, these latter co-existing with all manifestations of matter. Mr. Geo. de la Warr has demonstrated to us through his many researches the interdependence of Mind and Matter. The link between them is, as I believe, the paraphysical world, the world of the etheric, the world of Od or the Odic force, of such manifestations as ectoplasm and certain occult phenomena. This is the world which concerns the radiesthetist, the world through which he carries out his divinations, through which he can apprehend mental conceptions and physical matter. It is the world through which we may learn more about the underlying realities of our own planet—and of Heaven too!

D

Chapter 8

Some Factors in Case-Taking

The radiesthetic practitioner will learn by experience what tests he wants to make in working out a diagnosis. Often enough the condition he is treating will be obvious, which will avoid numerous tests he might otherwise wish to make. It may be a clinical case of influenza, of measles or appendicitis. On the other hand, one of the advantages of the radiesthetic method is that a subacute condition can often be detected before it has developed to the clinical stage. Where the radiesthetic method is especially apt is when the patient has no obvious disease, but feels ill and debilitated. His symptoms may be very real to himself, but inconclusive or meaningless to the practitioner. Radiesthesia does help us to find out what is really going on.

When a patient is treated for the first time, it will generally be advisable to make as full a radiesthetic analysis as possible. Often enough secondary factors will come to light which, whether or not they are contributing to the illness the patient is suffering from, may have important implications in his general health. An example of this is metal poisoning.

In radionic practice there are ten general disease conditions with their rates given on the Delawarr Cause Sheet, which may provide important information about the patient. These are:

1. Virus
2. Bacterium
3. Poison
4. Allergy
5. Toxins
6. Secretion imbalance
7. Hormone imbalance
8. Mineral imbalance
9. Vitamin imbalance
10. Psychological condition.

I almost always use 1, 2, 3, 5 and 10 when testing a case. On obtaining a reading of 55cm. on the rule for Virus, we should expect to find a high reading for one or other specific virus, such as common cold, influenza, encephalitis, or one of the epidemic virus diseases. If Poison comes out even slightly positive, even only 3cm. above the neutral reading of 45cm., we can add the rate for aluminium, thus having a composite rate of 90139799. If this rate gives a higher reading, then the patient is absorbing aluminium. Aluminium upsets the liver and the digestive system generally and Lycopodium will be found a very good remedy for eliminating the activated aluminium oxide. This may be better than giving Aluminium or Alumina in potency, especially if frequent checks as to dosage are not possible. Cadmium sulph. is a remedy which is also sometimes given. Tests can equally be made for lead and copper poisoning and other typical poisons for which rates are provided.

If Toxins give a positive reading, the rates for the different specific toxins can be employed to find which ones are operative. Sometimes, when the presence of a specific bacterium or virus is suspected, but its rate gives little indication of this, it is sound practice to test for the toxin. Supposing that 1, 2, 3, and 5 on the Cause Sheet all give a positive reading of, say, 55cm., it is possible that the rate for 10, Psychological Condition, will give a similar reading also. In that case the patient is probably suffering from nervous strain. As treatment proceeds and the readings for 1, 2, 3, and 5 are reduced to 45cm. or under, 10 should be reduced to a similar extent. If the reading for 10 gives a higher reading than those for the other general disease conditions, the patient is probably in a worried and nervous state, possibly with psychological implications. If with treatment the rate for 10 shows a reduction on the scale equally with the other general rates, we might assume that the patient is feeling comfortable and that the prescription is suiting him.

The sympathetic and parasympathetic nervous systems can be checked with S and P at 100cm. on the rule, usually giving a reading of 48–50cm. I think they can be more precisely checked on the triangle. A remedy which suits a patient at the time of testing will always bring S and P to 50cm. on the rule, or 0° on the triangle.

Urea and uric acid should never be forgotten. A high urea reading indicates toxaemia, invariably associated with infection of one kind or another, while a reading for uric acid higher than urea indicates uric acid poisoning and possibly a tendency to gout. Lycopodium is an excellent remedy for this condition. In an obvious case of gout we do, of course, think of Colchicum.

Sometimes the general disease rates 1, 2, 3, and 5 may all give a negative reaction (45cm. or lower), and yet a specific rate for a particular disease, such as 4031 for tuberculosis, may give a positive reading of 60cm. or more. This probably indicates a non-clinical subacute infection, which may nevertheless be affecting the patient's health. It could only be diagnosed through radiesthesia. If a patient is in the habit of treating himself homoeopathically, we may find that while the general disease rates are negative, we get several positive reactions for specific viruses and/or bacteria. This is the sort of eventuality which the practitioner must bear in mind.

As has already been indicated, where the patient is obviously not well, tests for specific organisms may not show anything very definite. On the triangle, with the use of witnesses, a whole number of tests may give a reading of 20° or 30°. The rates for toxins tested on the rule may provide the answer required. After an acute attack of influenza, the residual toxins may be the important condition to treat. The rates for gastric influenza and B. Typhosus coli are sometimes a valuable clue to a case. Arsenic alb. and Baptisia are commonly indicated for such affections.

Allopaths find it difficult to understand why different homoeopathic remedies are often needed to treat seemingly the same disease in different patients. This brings us, of course, to the basic principle of homoeopathy, that we should treat the patient and not the disease. Cinnamon is an excellent remedy for influenza, but sometimes Arsenic alb. or Baptisia may be the remedy that is clearly indicated. There may be many reasons for this, depending on the constitution of the patient, his medical history and his general condition at the time of testing. One reason may be that, with the invasion of the influenza virus, an old malarial infection has boiled up, as it may very well do. This will probably be a case of dealing with malarial toxins rather than the actual protozoon. Arsenic alb. is a leading remedy for malaria. In dealing with one of the typhoid group of bacteria, the patient may want Anacardium, Arsenic alb., Baptisia, Bryonia, or Kali mur. It may be found on test that Bryonia is also dealing with the pneumococcus organism or its toxins, or that Kali mur. is cutting out a positive reaction for B. Influenza.

In addition to Arsenic alb. and Cinnamon for influenza, other remedies often wanted are Aconite (which deals with catarrhals generally), Cadmium sulph. (said to be excellent for depression following influenza) and Gelsemium, which is also a remedy for measles, meningitis and whooping cough. Sulphur is a prime deep-acting homoeopathic remedy which deals with psora, i.e. a general unhealthy condition, possibly derived from hereditary factors or long-standing ill-health. It has a strong action on the liver and intestines and is also a skin remedy. It can sometimes turn the scale in a case of acute illness in which there is little reactive power, and should always be thought of in cases showing cancer reactions.

I would place Lycopodium and Sepia in very much the same category, all to be tested in cases of deep-seated disease. Rhus tox. and Sulphur are streptococcal remedies, while Hepar sulph. and Stannum met. deal with the staphylococcus. Where reactions are obtained for more than one infection and one remedy may be found on test to deal with all of them, we may infer that the infection which is ordinarily associated with the indicated remedy is the primary factor in the case—the nigger in the wood-pile. Get rid of that and the reactive power of the patient will quickly restore him to his normal level of health. We must not forget that a highly toxic case can give a number of positive reactions, and anything in the nature of an accurate diagnosis of basal causes can only be made after the disorganised state of the patient has been reduced to more normal proportions.

It will be realised that in using homoeopathic remedies, much will depend on the skill and acumen of the practitioner, especially in a difficult case. We can do something to codify treatment, and indeed I think we should do so, but in the last resort it is the resourcefulness of the practitioner which may decide whether the outcome is a successful one.

Consideration of radiesthesia and the homoeopathic remedy helps us to understand the nature of disease. All radiesthetic tests depend on *activation* and when we obtain a high reading, say, for streptococcus, we are detecting the streptococcal bacteria in a highly active state. We all know what a heavy cold feels like and it is easy to envisage the common cold virus and bacteria of catarrhal type multiplying fast and producing strong radiation. It is this intensity of radiation of the pathogenic organism which we endeavour to match with the potentised, or activated, remedy.

The action of this potentised remedy is easy to observe on the rule. Supposing we obtain a high reading for common cold virus in a patient and we give him one dose of Aconitum 6. We will find very soon afterwards that the reading has been reduced. But if we give a dose of Aconitum 30, the reading should drop a good deal further. If the 30c potency is exactly right, we will for the moment have knocked out the intensity, or activated condition, of the virus with the potentised remedy. Assuming that the virus represents an acute infection, it will soon regain a fair degree of virulence. Thus we have the need for a repetition of doses—a series of knocks.

Through radiesthesia we are able to discover what potency or remedy we require in each case. Too high a potency may upset the nervous balance of the patient and spoil the treatment. It could in an extreme case cause collapse. The object must be to maintain and fortify the vitality and nervous balance of the patient, while dealing at the same time with the disease.

Often enough a remedy in the 6 or 12 potency will be needed. A 6c potency has an energy level corresponding closely to the general energy level of a normal human being. So a series of 'taps' with a 6c remedy may do better than a higher potency would do. In any case, where the higher potency is employed, very much fewer doses will be required than would be the case with a 6c remedy, and they would be more widely spaced out. Once the intensity of the disease has been reduced to the lowest terms, continuation of the treatment might be expected to over-stimulate the patient and complicate the case. This is why patients are advised to stop taking remedies once improvement has set in. Really high potencies are generally prescribed one dose at a time with instructions not to repeat it except after an interval of one week or more, unless the one dose is considered sufficient. The best way of administering high, or fairly high, potencies, say from 1,000 upwards, is to test each dose before it is given. Although high potencies have been known to bring about spectacular and rapid cures, the inexperienced would be wise to keep to potencies not higher than 6 or 12.

While the action of 6c and higher potencies produces something which might be likened to an electric shock, a vibration which syntonises with that of the disease for which it was given, at the same time retaining the *effect* of the drug from which it was originally prepared, the action of a low-potency 3x remedy is more like the action of an allopathic remedy whose effect depends on chemical reaction. It can be repeated with comparative impunity.

A remedy which illustrates well the importance of potencies is Ruta. Ruta acts on joints and the periosteum, or covering of bones. It is also a rectal remedy. Supposing we are treating a strained wrist with Ruta. If we gave Ruta 6 in repetition, a sensitive patient would in time very probably begin to complain of tightness and pain in the rectum and the muscles of his back might become uncomfortably contracted. On the other hand Ruta 3x would act more like an allopathic remedy and affect directly the damaged periosteum and tendons without over-stimulating nerves and muscles. And indeed, on test, if the rate for 'inflammation of wrist' were set on the instrument, the 3x potency of Ruta would in all probability be the one indicated. This could be repeated in a succession of doses in a way that a higher potency could not. We must understand therefore that while 6c and higher potencies deal effectively with the pathogenic micro-organism, low potency 3x remedies may be needed to eliminate residual toxins, tone up organic tissue and restore organs to normal activity. It may even be found, shall we say, in an elderly person of low vitality, that treatment with 3x remedies alone is indicated.

In taking on a new case, it is only a matter of minutes to check the patient for the more ordinary diseases from which the human race suffers, albeit so often in subacute form. We should not forget the miasmatic diseases such as syphilis, gonorrhoea, tuberculosis and cancer, checked if necessary with the rates for their toxins, and such conditions as anaemia, diabetes, fibroma, tumour, etc., depending on the nature of the case. The rates for toxaemia and septicaemia are useful aids to a complete analysis.

Now a word about dosage. Supposing that we have decided to prescribe a remedy in the 6c potency. If it is really well suited to the patient and constitutional to him at the time of test, we should expect to get a reading of about 70° or more on the triangle. Sizing up the case and taking into account the age and sensitivity of the patient, we shall have an idea of what the dosage should be. We should certainly assume that the remedy could be repeated for several days for, apart from other considerations, only repetitive doses will reduce the reading to something near 0°. If the potency were higher, the number of doses would be less, while low-potency 3x remedies could be prescribed either alone or in conjunction with higher potencies. As with low potencies we are working on the tissue level, i.e. the action is comparable with the chemical action of non-potentised remedies, the number of tablets to a dose is a matter to consider and often enough the measure will be two tablets to a dose.

It is common practice among radiesthetists, and indeed radionic practitioners also, to rely on the psychic method to decide dosage, and for this some kind of diagram or chart is often useful. Such a diagram helps us to concentrate on the problem and one that I devised for myself is reproduced. Supposing for argument's sake that the prescription in a particular case is Aconite and Sulphur (which go well together) in the 6c potency and Lycopodium and Nux vomica in the 3x potency. With the patient's specimen at A and samples of Aconite 6 and Sulphur 6 at B, and with the diagram laid in front of the operator covering the lower half of the triangle, we hold the pendulum over the left-hand circle at the top of the diagram signifiying 'Once a Day'. We can repeat this over the middle and the right-hand circles and note the pendulum reaction in each case, leaving it to the pendulum (as it were) to decide by the reactions obtained what the daily dosage should be. Having discovered this, we then move the pendulum along the scale in the middle of the diagram to find out how many days the prescription should last. Ordinarily we might expect it to be 10, 14 or even 21 days.

We repeat the above process with the two 3x remedies at B, but first decide the number of tablets to a dose, using the bottom scale on the diagram. It must be understood that to what extent the resulting dosage is correct depends very much on the knowledge and experience of the practitioner. But where, for instance, he cannot make up his mind whether a remedy should be given twice or three times a day, the pendulum should decide the point for him.

I should make it clear that there is no special advantage in using the diagram reproduced. The individual must decide for himself how best he can make such tests at the psychic level and what kind of diagram he prefers—if he uses one at all. One likes to think of his

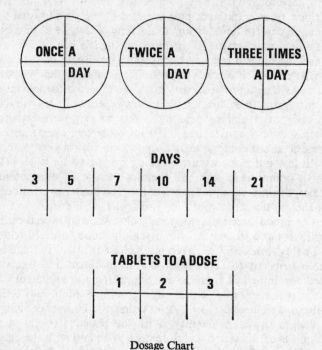

Dosage Chart

brain acting as a kind of computer, which arrives at the correct answer after his current tests and past knowledge and experience bearing on the case in hand have all been taken into account. There is the belief, probably shared by many practitioners, that information can come to the radiesthetist in such prospections from a source entirely outside of himself or from some level of his unconscious mind. For practical purposes it is best in my opinion just to ask the pendulum for the answer, without speculating too much as to how it is arrived at.

Chapter 9

Actual Cases

Having gone over the several methods open to us for making a diagnosis and working out a prescription, I thought it would help the reader to understand these methods better if a few examples of actual cases were given. These cases are based on my own limited practice, taken more or less at random, but chosen as far as possible to show how a particular method can be selected to meet a particular situation.

It is not always easy to ascertain with any degree of accuracy what organisms are affecting a patient and, in order to do this, different methods may suit different cases best. For instance, when working with the rule-cum-vial connection arrangement and setting up in turn rates for the different virus or microbial infections on the instrument, we may begin by obtaining only negative reactions with readings of 45cm., or under. And then, by setting up a rate for, say, Streptococcus viridans, the pendulum may travel right up the rule to near the 100cm. mark, indicating acute streptococcal infection. This may be the only positive reaction arrived at and, if this is so, it is something very definite and precise to work on.

In another case all rule readings for disease conditions tested may show negative, or only very slightly positive reactions, and in such a subacute case it may be good practice to test the various nosodes on the P polarity. One or two nosodes may reduce the reading to well below 10cm., indicating in a very definite manner what organisms, or their toxins, are affecting the health of the patient. It is, of course, equally open to the practitioner to begin testing his patient's specimen on the triangle, and this may give the information required. But in cases of doubt he can always check his results on the rule. For testing remedies to treat a specific infection, the triangle is undoubtedly a very good way of matching the remedy exactly to the disease. But it may be wise to go back to the rule for checking the potency on the P polarity, or in any other way which suggests itself to the practitioner.

It should be emphasised that the following cases should not be taken as textbook examples showing how a particular condition or disease should be treated. It would be wrong for me to attempt to carry out any such task. They are simply meant to help the practitioner new to radiesthesia to discover ways in which he can best help his patients. It is for him to decide what methods to adopt and precisely how to go about getting out his prescription.

I have purposely avoided discussion of the sort of acute cases which general practitioners meet daily in their practice, as it is the methods I wish to discuss and not the diseases. Once the practitioner has mastered his methods, he should be in a position to tackle whatever case he meets with every prospect of being able to treat it homoeopathically with confidence. Nevertheless, as his technique improves, he will come to realise progressively that it is the chronic subacute cases, those which do not respond to standard methods of treatment, which can be so often helped through a sound combination of radiesthesia and homoeopathy. It is the chronic intractable cases which make a study of radiesthesia so very much worth while.

A general check-up

The patient is a homoeopath and has suffered from heart symptoms. Requires a check-up. The 'General Disease Conditions' (see p. 50) are all low. 1, 2, 3, and 4 are 40cm., toxins (No. 5) are 38cm. With such readings we might assume that the patient has been treating himself. Heart is 48–41, the figure 48 referring to function (49–50 is normal) and 41 to inflammation or toxic condition, a negative reading (45 is normal). Deficiency of heart is also 41. Heart muscle gives similar readings and other rates for heart such as aneurism give 40, but tachycardia gives 43—still a negative reading, though slightly positive as compared with the other readings. This is not of much significance. The organs measured up very well. Polarity 39–39/39, urea and uric acid 40.

Decided to check for infection on the rule with vial connection and nosodes, using the rate for toxins, which gave a reading of 38. Each nosode was placed in turn alongside the 100cm. mark, with the nosode on one side on a rubber block and a sample of S on the other. When working on the rule this method of employing nosodes is sometimes useful. It is quick and avoids putting up individual rates. Moreover, subacute infections are easily detected as the pendulum is very sensitive to nosode reaction. The tests must be made on a rate giving a fairly low reading, as there is then plenty of room on the scale for getting differentiated readings. In the present case positive reactions can be found between 45 and 100cm., giving the largest range possible on the rule. Readings for a nosode at or below 50–55cm. are probably of minimal significance and, depending to some extent on other readings, can be disregarded.

The results were as follows:

Tests on rule-cum-vial connection with nosodes

Influenza virus, Asian	85 cm.
Encephalitis	75
Streptococcus haemolyticus	90
Streptococcus viridans	95
Staphylococcus	90
B. Typhosus coli	90
Typhoid	80
Paratyphoid	85
Dysentery	90
B. coli	90

It may be of value to compare the above results with readings obtained by putting up the rates for the various infections.

Tests with specific rates

Influenza virus A	75 cm.
Influenza virus B	70
Influenza virus, Asian	85
Streptococcus viridans	90
Staphylococcus	90
Typhoid	90
Paratyphoid	90
Dysentery	85
Common cold virus	90

We can conclude from these two sets of readings that in fact the infections are very active despite the low readings for General Disease Conditions, good organ readings and balanced polarity readings (all 39cm.). It would appear that the patient has been keeping himself fairly fit by his own efforts, even if he has not succeeded in eliminating specific organisms, or their toxins.

Again, to make the comparison complete, we can test on the triangle with witnesses or nosodes.

Tests on triangle with Turenne witnesses

Influenza	40 degrees
Staphylococcus	40
Streptococcus	30
Typhoid	30
Paratyphoid	40
B. coli	40
Dysentery	30
(Endocarditis)	(0)

Other witnesses gave very low readings, some of only 0°. One would not expect this if the patient had not been treating himself.

It was found by testing on the triangle that three remedies in the 6c potency normalised all readings. Rhus tox. is a great streptococcal remedy and is also a septic remedy. Stannum met. is a valuable staphylococcal remedy and Gelsemium is an influenza remedy. These three remedies went well together and were given twice a day for twenty-one days. It should be realised that a remedy can deal effectively with the toxins of a specific organism even if it is not a recognised remedy for dealing with the organism itself.

Where there is no organic disease of an organ such as the heart, heart symptoms can generally be traced to the presence in the system of inimical pathogens. The heart is especially vulnerable to the streptococcus. If we had been particularly concerned to find what bacteria were affecting the heart when testing with the rule-cum-vial connection with nosodes, we could have used the rate for 'inflammation of heart' instead of that for toxins. In a duodenal case we would have tested on the rate for duodenum, unless of course the rate for 'inflammation of duodenum' gave a high reading. In that case, instead of placing each nosode alongside the vial connection at 100cm., it could be placed alongside the specimen at 0cm. We should then find that nosodes representing pathogens affecting the duodenum would reduce the reading to 10cm., or below. This in fact may be a more exact test.

Colds and influenza

The climate of Britain makes her inhabitants very susceptible to catarrh, colds and influenza. There are a number of homoeopathic remedies which deal with these conditions. Aconite, Arsenic alb., Baptisia, Cinnamon, Gelsemium and Rhus tox. are all good for colds and influenza. Calcarea carb. and Sabadilla deal with catarrh. Pulsatilla acts on mucous membranes and can be useful in catarrhal conditions. In an epidemic attack of influenza we can expect to find a general invasion of pathogenic organisms such a B. coli (in its invasion form), Streptococcus and Pneumococcus, the typhoid group of organisms, in addition to common cold virus and the catarrhals.

It is easy to see why different cases of influenza need different remedies. Baptisia will in all probability be indicated where B. Typhosus coli is present. Arsenic alb. may be required in a case in which the toxins of an old malarial infection have become active. Rhus tox. will probably be needed to deal with streptococcal infection, perhaps in addition to the toxins of a typhoid infection. Pulsatilla is a leading remedy for tuberculosis and may be useful in clearing up T.B. toxins. Different strains may require different drugs to obtain optimum results, and finally the constitution of the patient may be the deciding factor as to which of two or more remedies is best.

A patient apparently affected by several infections may respond very well to only one remedy. So much depends on the vitality of the patient, his general constitution and such factors as, for instance, the condition of the intestinal tract. Of the several positive infections revealed on test, one or more may be of considerably greater importance than the rest. Treat them, and the patient recovers! On the other hand, painstaking work on rule or triangle may be largely abortive if one organism affecting the patient badly is not detected and treated specifically. As an example, an acute B. Welchii infection can be very upsetting to a patient, whatever else is wrong with him, unless it is treated specifically. What is certain is that a remedy which is really going to help a patient materially must be constitutional to that patient at the moment of testing. It must be well indicated by such general tests as that on the P polarity rule reading, or on the sympathetic nervous system as tested on the triangle.

Supposing that we have a case in which general tests give good readings, where the polarity is normal and urea and uric acid are negative. But the patient feels debilitated and complains that she has a cold and head noises. We know that she has been treating herself, probably to very good effect, but she feels the need of expert assistance.

In our tests we may find a high reading for Influenza virus A. Supposing it gives a rule-cum-instrument reading with the vial connection of 90cm. Cinnamon is a very good remedy for influenza, and Cinnamon 6 placed alongside the specimen at 0cm. may reduce the reading to below 10cm. On the other hand Cinnamon 30 may be needed. If we consider high potencies, Cinnamon CM may reduce the reading to below 10cm., but it would be all the more important to test it in other ways also, such as on the P polarity reading.

Let us assume that the patient wants Cinnamon 30. If that is so and it is really a good remedy for the patient at the time of testing, it should take the R reading right up the scale to 70cm. or above. This reading will be obtained by placing the remedy alongside the specimen at 0cm. with nothing else on the rule. As an additional check we can *start* the pendulum oscillating at 100cm. and bring it down the scale (with the remedy still alongside the specimen at 0cm.), when we should feel a resistance before the 95cm. mark is reached. We might then find that the pendulum balances at 98–100cm.

If we had done the testing on the triangle, we should expect to find a reading of, say, 70° or more with the specimen at A and Cinnamon 30 at B. A witness of Influenza virus A placed at B would equally give a high reading, say 70°–90°. If Cinnamon 30 is the correct remedy, this placed at B, but just outside the circle, would return the pendulum to 0°. We can also test Cinnamon 30 on S and P (i.e. on the sympathetic and parasympathetic nervous system) placed successively at B. A further test would be to place the remedy at B and S and P in turn at C. In each case the pendulum should oscillate along CD.

It is far more likely than not in a case of influenza that the patient's system is invaded by a number of micro-organisms and we can test it in the following way on the rule. We can first find out what the P polarity reading is. Supposing it is 43cm. We can then test various nosodes alongside the specimen and find which reduce the reading to below 10cm. We may obtain in this way reactions for Influenza virus Asian, poliomyelitis, streptococcus and B. Typhosus coli. This at once suggests several remedies. Rhus tox. is a great remedy for Streptococcus and Baptisia for B. Typhosus coli, while Gelsemium deals with the influenza virus and with poliomyelitis. It is not unusual to obtain a reaction for poliomyelitis in a case of influenza or a severe cold. This may be an actual infection or the activation of old toxins. It is recognised that a patient may quite easily have a mild attack of poliomyelitis without knowing it.

We next test the likely remedies on the P polarity. We shall probably find that the three remedies mentioned are all well indicated. We might find other remedies equally well indicated. Aconitum n. could easily be one of them and, being an excellent remedy for the common cold virus and catarrhal conditions generally, it would be for the practitioner to decide whether it should be included in the prescription. It is, of course, an excellent remedy for reducing temperature, but should only be given if properly indicated. All remedies chosen could then be tested together on the rule on the P polarity and vitality readings.

If one has to decide between two or three remedies to deal with a particular infection, we can proceed as follows. We chose Rhus tox. for streptococcus, but it is possible that Sulphur or even Lycopodium might be better in an individual case. We can test these remedies in the following way.

Place the Streptococcus 30 nosode on the 100cm. mark with a sample of S alongside it on the rubber block. We should obtain a reading of about 5cm. Now place Rhus tox., Lycopodium and Sulphur, in whatever potency has been chosen, in turn alongside the specimen. The remedy which increases the reading most will be the most suitable. Supposing Rhus tox. gives a reading of 25cm. If we now add Cinnamon to the Rhus tox., and if the two drugs go well together, the reading will go higher by a limited amount. On test the Cinnamon removes the radiation of influenza from the patient, which allows the Rhus tox. to have a greater effect in killing off the streptococcus. This could equally be argued the other way round.

It is often possible to obtain a remedy which will deal with more than one infection giving a positive reading. Sometimes a remedy indicated strongly for an infection or condition, which is obviously an important factor in the case, will be found to deal with other infections giving positive reactions, with which the remedy is not ordinarily associated. In this case we can assume that we are dealing with toxins rather than live pathogens.

When we place a nosode at 100cm. with S in radiative contact with it and with a patient's specimen at 0cm., a low reading, say of under 15cm., suggests that the organism represented by the nosode is active in the patient. I have previously described this type of test as a test for 'Deficiency'. A low reading of 10cm. or under does suggest very definitely that the nosode, or a comparable remedy, would be effective in eliminating the organism from the patient's system. In a similar manner a low reading for a remedy suggests it as being wanted to help balance up the sum total of the patient's vitality, or general nerve balance.

A question of potency

This straightforward case exemplifies how the right potency can be arrived at. The patient was feeling very unwell, and as her next-door neighbour had been in bed for a week, she wanted to avoid the possibility of following her to a similar state of inactivity. The readings I recorded were:

General disease conditions

1. 34
2. 33   Polarity 38–38/38
3. 35
5. 35

30c nosodes tested on the P polarity

	cm.
Influenza	15
Influenza virus A	8
Influenza virus B	12
Influenza Asian	12
Streptococcus haemolyticus	8
Typhoid	8
Paratyphoid	8
Poliomyelitis	9
B. Morgan	10

It was obvious from the readings, and indeed the patient, that she had been attempting to treat herself. Otherwise we would expect at least some of the General Disease Conditions listed to be positive, i.e. over 45cm., and the P polarity to be something higher than 38cm.

Each nosode was placed in turn alongside the specimen at 0cm. on one rubber block, a sample of P (acetylcholine) being placed on the other side of the specimen on another rubber block. The patient was obviously suffering from an attack of Influenza virus A, this giving the lowest reading of the influenzas tested. As previously stated, poliomyelitis is sometimes found in an influenzal attack, which may be the activation of old toxins rather than a new infection.

Having found the offending pathogens, appropriate remedies were found by testing the nosodes on the triangle. The patient's specimen was placed at A and each nosode in turn placed at B. Likely remedies were placed in turn alongside the nosodes, but just outside the circle. At first 6c remedies were tested. Gelsemium 6 corrected the reading for Influenza virus A, and indeed all the influenzal readings, bringing the pendulum into oscillation along CD. Gelsemium 6 normalised poliomyelitis and also the readings for Typhoid and Paratyphoid. Sulphur is *the* remedy for B. Morgan and was indicated as the right choice in a similar manner.

The next step was to test these remedies in the 30c potency on the triangle, and these also brought the nosode readings up to 0°, with the pendulum oscillating along CD. These two remedies were then tested in both potencies on the P polarity rule readings and the 30c remedies gave the lower readings, say about 5cm. The pendulum decided the dosage as one tablet of each remedy in the 30c potency twice a day for eight days. This proved to be exactly right. For just before the patient had finished the remedies, they were still giving a very low reading on the P polarity. But after she had finished them, with the same remedies tested again on the P polarity, the readings had risen to something like 12 or 15cm. All this time the patient had carried on with her daily activities, although naturally not feeling her best. If she had been given 6c remedies, she might have had to take to her bed and, in any case, her recovery would have taken a good deal longer.

When I first tested this patient, her liver gave a very bad reading on the triangle, something like 50°, and I prescribed Arnica 3x, Lycopodium 3x and Nux Vomica 3x, two tablets of each t.d.s. for eight days to tone up the liver and gastro-intestinal tract, Arnica being included to reduce toxins and tone up the nervous system. These three remedies were tested on the P polarity. After about five days of the treatment, the patient still complained of internal discomfort and asked me to check the prescription. The 30c remedies

Vial connection employed for testing human specimen on rule at 0cm., with waveform provided by instrument

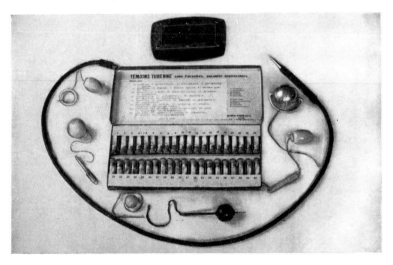

Box of Turenne witnesses, Delawarr portable detector with probe, an original red Bovis pendulum, a metal 'Universal' pendulum and several pendulums of whale ivory

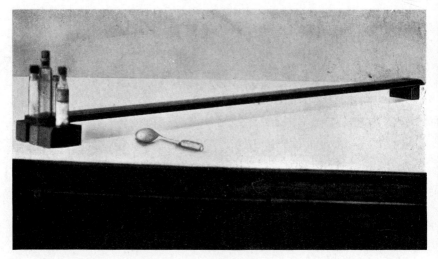

A patient's specimen is tested on the P polarity at 0cm. on the rule with the remedy on one side and P (acetylcholine) on the other, placed on rubber blocks. A pendulum lies on the table

were still very much wanted, but the 3x remedies were no longer so well indicated on the *P* polarity. The liver and other organs were much improved. So I substituted Bryonia 3x and Sabadilla 3x, both tested on the *P* polarity and intended to deal more directly with infections rather than organs. At a still later stage, when the 30c remedies were finished, Bryonia 6 was prescribed together with the two 3x remedies, which soon brought full recovery. Bryonia deals with the typhoid group of pathogens among others and Sabadilla is often useful in cases of colds and catarrh.

I have given this case in full detail as it was essentially a straight-forward one, each stage of which should be easily followed by the reader. Testing in this way on the *P* polarity with nosodes sometimes gives better indications in my opinion of the active infections present than other methods, whether on rule or triangle. It also gives better indications of deep-seated toxins present in subacute chronic cases of long standing.

Catarrh

This is just another case, somewhat similar to the above, of a new and elderly patient living abroad, who asked me to check her readings and complained simply of catarrh! The readings were as follows:

General disease conditions	Rule readings	cm.
1. 45	Urea and uric acid	47
2. 44	Septicaemia	46
3. 44	Acidity	45
4. 45	Bone	49–48
5. 47	Brain	50–43
6. 47		
7. 47	Nosodes tested on *P* polarity	
8. 47		cm.
9. 43	Streptococcus H.	10
10. 42	Typhoid	5
	B. Morgan	8

Readings on the triangle

	degrees		degrees
Streptococcus co.	30	Duodenum	30
Streptococcus H.	60	Rectum	30
Typhoid	40	Lungs	30
B. Morgan	40	Oesophagus	30
		Kidneys	30
Polarity	39–39/39	Pancreas	30
		Arteriosclerosis	30

From what the patient said in her letter, or rather did not say, the case was obviously of a chronic subacute character. The polarity suggests a slightly inflammatory condition (38cm. being the normal for the three readings on my rule), and the readings for urea and uric acid, both slightly positive, indicate very definite infection. No. 2 of the General Disease Conditions for bacterial infection is actually 1cm. below the normal balance point of 45cm., which suggests that the patient had already been having treatment to whatever extent, very possibly treating herself. In any case the G.D.C. should only be taken as pointers to obtaining a correct overall picture. No. 10 of the G.D.C. is 42cm., below all the other G.D.C. readings, which suggests that the patient was psychologically well balanced at the time and not unduly disturbed about her health. The remedies, tested in the same way as in the former case, came out as:

Baptisia 6
Rhus tox. 6 } One table of each t.d.s., a.c., for 14 days.

These two remedies, tested together, corrected the readings for infections on the triangle. Sulphur was not indicated in this case for treating B. Morgan, which may have been a case of toxins rather than an actual live infection. We should accept the fact that absolute precision by way of diagnosis in these tests is something we can seldom achieve. The body is far too complex in its working. This equally applies to many orthodox tests. From the point of view of treatment, however, we should be able to obtain all we need to know.

Trauma and shock

Every accident, whether major or minor, is accompanied by shock. So wrote the late Dr. Dorothy Shepherd. And the great remedy for shock is Arnica. I remember reading in a newspaper during the Second World War of a young woman who had been caught in some falling masonry as a result of an air raid. Although badly hurt, she showed remarkable courage and joked with the Civil Defence personnel who were trying to reach her. Eventually a doctor was able to get to her and he gave her an injection of morphia. She died very soon afterwards. I have sometimes wondered since whether a dose of Arnica in potency would have carried her through and saved her life, with perhaps the addition of Hypericum to reduce pain.

In cases of severe shock the usual procedure is to give blood transfusions. Dr. Shepherd thought that Arnica would often do as well, if not better. She believed on deep moral grounds that blood transfusions should be avoided whenever possible. It may well be that Arnica could sometimes take the place of blood transfusions, except in cases where there has been extensive bleeding.*

People often suffer from shock without knowing it and sometimes long after the event which caused it. It is an easy matter to check a patient for shock on a radionic instrument. Persons of weakly constitution can suffer shock effects for weeks following an accident, or even after they have strained themselves from over-exertion. Sometimes manipulative treatment can produce unpleasant shock symptoms, when the nervous system suffers and the patient becomes extremely debilitated.

Take the case of a person who, from whatever cause, has seemingly lost all reactive power, feels cold and miserable and is forced to spend a good deal of his time lying down. If he has been in an accident, he may even suffer from slight concussion and know what damaged brain tissue feels like. I once experienced this condition myself, although in a very mild form. It is extremely unpleasant.

It is an advantage in dealing with a badly debilitated patient suffering from shock if each dose of Arnica can be tested separately. Some practitioners might start with a high potency of Arnica, such as a CM. A practitioner with limited experience of homoeopathy might do better in going no higher than 30c. To start with Arnica 30 may bring the reading for shock right down the scale to below 10cm. If every dose of Arnica is only given when it cuts out shock as represented by its rate and brings the reading right down the scale, this will ensure that the patient's vitality is nursed back to its normal level without any aggravations or setbacks. Every little bit of his vitality will be safeguarded and gradually augmented as treatment proceeds. And every test will indicate which potency is required.

Trauma can be treated in much the same way. Arnica can be tested on the trauma or the shock rate, according to which gives the higher reading. Where there is obvious physical injury other remedies such as Hypericum, Ledum, Rhus tox. and Ruta may be needed. If it is suspected that the brain is affected, the rate for trauma or shock can be put up on the instrument followed by the rate for brain. A good positive reading can sometimes be obtained by adding the rate for bone to that for shock or trauma.

It will be found sometimes that doses of Arnica 3x and some higher potency of the same remedy can be given together. The lower potency will act more directly on the damaged tissues. With physical injury repetitive doses of Arnica 3x will probably be wanted, in addition to whatever is needed in higher potencies as tested. Where the brain is damaged an alternative remedy is Natrum sulph.

* See p. 36 in *Homoeopathy for the First-Aider*, by Dr. Dorothy Shepherd (Health Science Press).

Dr. Shepherd, who wrote several well-known books on homoeo-pathy, never gave us anything better than *Homoeopathy for the First-Aider*. With this book as a guide and radiesthesia to indicate what potencies are needed—of vital importance where shock is severe—the practitioner should feel well equipped to deal with whatever cases of shock and trauma come his way.

On the one occasion when I suffered minor shock myself as a result of a manipulation and owing to the state of health I was in at the time, it was all I could do to walk to the post. I had a most unpleasant feeling of fragility and had to spend a good deal of time on my back. I gradually regained my strength by taking carefully checked doses of Arnica. Even so, it took me a month to get back to normal. At such times nothing can take the place of Arnica.

If one has no radionic instrument, doses of Arnica can equally well be tested on the rule on the P polarity. If we start giving Arnica 30, say every six hours, the time will soon come when the reading which the drug provides on the P polarity will go above 10cm. We can then drop down to Arnica 6 and finally (if necessary), to clear up the case, Arnica 3x.

Headaches

Headache is a common complaint which can be brought on through various causes, not excluding psychological or mental stress. Some-times the explanation is simple and the cause easily removed. Take the case of an active and healthy woman, who has recently been complaining of headaches. Without much testing, two virus infec-tions showed up positive on the triangle, encephalitis and poliomye-litis, which both showed 40°. Ideally, a remedy which will correct an infection on the triangle and produce a reading of 90° when tested by itself against the specimen, will also return lesser readings for other infections to 0°. The general run of tests for the various specific infections will seldom give a reading of 0°. A reading of something like 15° to 20° is much more likely. A whole series of tests for various virus and bacterial infections may give a reading of, say, 20°. If one then gets a reading of 40°, 50° or higher, it is significant. We can assume that the lesser readings refer to toxins in the system of the patient. In the case under consideration Calcarea phos. 6x and Hepar sulph. 6 were indicated, dosage being one tablet of each t.d.s., a.c. for fourteen days. This cleared up the headaches. Calcarea phos. is a remedy to be thought of in some virus infections. I have no record as to why Hepar sulph. was chosen, but it is a headache remedy and must have proved suitable on test.

Another case of persistent headaches in an active middle-aged woman, for which no cure had been found, gave the following readings, this time on the rule:

General disease conditions

1. 40		Urea	35
2. 42		Uric acid	40
3. 60		Brain	48–90
		Bone	46–90
Polarity			37–37/37
Aluminium poisoning (90139799)			80
Aluminium (39799)			70
Nerves			$47\frac{1}{2}$–70

Pineal, thyroid, pituitary and suprarenal glands were out of balance.

These few readings are sufficient evidence that the nervous system was badly impaired, the readings for brain and bone inflammation being particularly bad, as also that for nerves. At the same time no active infection was found and indeed readings for urea, uric acid and the polarity confirmed that general toxaemia was no part of the case. On the other hand General Disease Condition No. 3 for poisons was high and aluminium poisoning gave a very high reading. It should also be noted that uric acid gave a slightly higher reading than urea, although both are negative considered as disease conditions.

Lycopodium is a very good remedy for eliminating aluminium and Lycopodium 6 reduced the reading for it to a very low point on the rule—below 10cm. Of other remedies tested I found that Calcarea carb. 6 dealt effectively with the brain and bone inflammation and these two remedies together normalised all bad readings on test. I think one can assume by this that calcium metabolism was faulty, which was corrected by Calcarea carb 6. Lycopodium is a deep-acting remedy, it contains Silica, acts on bone, is often useful for stimulating the suprarenal gland and has a symptomatology which covers a wide range of action. The prescription was:

Calcarea carb. 6 ⎫
Lycopodium 6   ⎬ M.50. One of each t.d.s., a.c.
               ⎭

The prescription lasted for seventeen days, after which I got an enthusiastic report. The headaches had either gone or been reduced to minimal proportions.

In all cases of headache brain, bone and endocrines should always be tested, in addition to whatever seems required in the way of a general analysis. It is very possible that inflammation of spinal cord and general nerves will come out positive.

Malaria

An advantage of the radiesthetic method is that tests can easily be made for infections which would not ordinarily be expected to occur in persons living in Britain. But the unexpected can quite easily happen, and in making a comprehensive analysis we ignore routine testing at our peril. Thus it is that, unless we know what the trouble is with which we have to deal, it may be advisable to test for malaria.

This was brought home to me in a very convincing way. When I first came to live in Weybridge I did a certain amount of gardening, including work close to the broken soil. I was bitten badly on two or three occasions by mosquitoes, but ignored this. It was some time afterwards when I obtained a strong reaction for malaria. I was perspiring a good deal at the time, especially in the morning.

Shortly after this I asked a medical friend of mine, a brilliant radiesthetist, to check my specimen. He wrote complimenting me on my unexpected finding, but thought it must be a matter of malarial toxins rather than an actual infection by the protozoon, however mild. At about this time there was a paragraph in the local paper stating how disturbed the authorities at Woking were at the poisonous nature of the mosquitoes in the district, one breed of which was definitely malarial.

It was many years since I had made passing visits to malarial countries without any trouble, and there is no doubt in my mind that I contracted a very mild dose of malaria from the mosquitoes in my garden. That is not surprising considering the number of Army men, who were abroad during the war, who are normally billeted in parts of Surrey. Not long after this I had to tell an elderly patient in the neighbourhood that I obtained a reaction for malaria. He wrote back that he had found several mosquitoes in his bed!

My first indication that I had a malarial infection was by testing myself on the rule with the rate for malaria set on the instrument, which gave a reading of something like 70cm. The next thing that one can do is to test for malarial toxins. I recall that my doctor friend got a reading of something like 90° on his triangle, indicating an acute infection. But, of course, the malarial strain in a British mosquito cannot be compared with that found in tropical countries.

Sometimes a reaction for malaria is found in patients suffering from an attack of influenza and in those who have lived abroad in tropical or semi-tropical countries. Remedies must be found to reduce the readings on the rule to below 10cm., or to normalise the readings on the triangle at 0°. Two leading remedies for this condition are Arsenic alb. and Chininium sulph. Another good remedy is Malaria officinalis, which consists of decomposed vegetable matter. When the readings have been normalised, it may be advisable to give a course of one or more low potency 3x or even 1x remedies to try to ensure that both the protozoon and its toxins are finally eliminated. The toxins, unless completely eliminated, have a habit of boiling up during an attack of heavy cold or influenza—especially, it seems, in the spring.

Persistent and excessive perspiration is very unpleasant to live with. In fat people it may be necessary to attend to the diet and check the endocrines, especially the thyroid, and calcium metabolism. Remedies can be tested on the rate for 'excessive fat'. Often enough an infection will be found to be the cause of perspiration. Aconite n. and Arsenic alb. are two leading remedies for inflammatory conditions, for colds, catarrh and influenza. When dealing with viruses such as encephalitis, the more unusual form of Aconite lycotonum may be a better remedy.

Arsenic alb. in low potency can be very helpful in acutely febrile cases, but I sometimes prefer the 5x potency to 3x. The concentration of the drug in Arsenic alb. 3x requires that it be labelled 'Poison'. In this form it is a powerful quick-acting drug and bears little repetition. The same applies to Arsenic iod. I do not think anything stronger than 5x potency for these two remedies is usually required.

Where perspiration is heavy, with or without a temperature, it may be advisable to check for the Brucella group of infections, which come under the heading of undulant fever. Humans are generally infected in northern countries from a bovine strain.

Parasites

Of the cases I have examined, I have been surprised at the proportion which were affected by parasites. Often enough the patient has no idea that he is so affected, but parasites can be very detrimental to health. They cause general toxaemia and will often provide a high reading when the patient is tested on the rate for septicaemia. In a bad case it is not uncommon to obtain positive reactions for one or more of the miasmatic diseases, syphilis, gonorrhoea, tuberculosis, and even cancer. The inference to be drawn from these readings is that the system is badly disorganised by the poisonous nature of the parasites and the gross toxaemia present, and not necessarily that he has contracted any one of these diseases.

Parasitic infection in England is generally caused by eating insufficiently washed salads or infected meat, which is generally pig-meat in some form or other. There are a number of classified parasites and I myself have a round dozen of witnesses of specific parasites. Nevertheless I think it is very difficult to ascertain through

Parasites

radiesthesia exactly what the parasitic infection in a particular case consists of. One type of infection may come out very positive, but there may be one or more others present which are comparatively dormant. A physiotherapist friend, who gives colonic irrigations, has told me that it is usual for only one type of developed parasite to be found in the stool. Assuming it is a worm that we are treating, it is important from the treatment point of view to decide whether the parasite is a tape worm or some other form of worm. There are several rates provided by the Delawarr Laboratories which should normally give sufficient evidence of parasites for the purpose of treatment. These are:

Worms	9052
Parasites	80810
Parasitic toxins	70088
Ascarides	102
Tape worm	20458
Ringworm (fungus)	8071

The Drown rate of 8046 for taenia may also be useful. A positive reading for parasitic toxins is a good indication of the presence of parasites, which can be checked with other parasitic rates. If we add the rate for an organ such as the colon, small intestine, etc., to that of parasites, worms or parasitic toxins, and obtain a higher reading than that for parasites or their toxins alone, that is a confirmatory test. It also shows which organs are infected. In a bad case a good deal of toxaemia (tested with the rate for inflammation) will be found in such organs as the liver, colon, small intestines, caecum and appendix, and quite probably in the stomach and bladder also.

There is a very good remedy for worms, which deals effectively with tape worms, and this is Cuprum oxy. nig. plus Antimony crud. In 1x form it is fairly toxic, but it may be very necessary. It can also be had in 3x potency. It is important to get the dosage right and for this I proceed with the vial connection arrangement as follows.

I place the patient's specimen on a watch glass at 0cm. on the rule and put up the rate for worms into small intestine (905222) on the instrument, or whatever parasitic rate gives the highest reading. Having found which potency is indicated, I place one tablet of the remedy on the watch glass with the specimen and find to what extent the reading is reduced. I then add one tablet at a time until the reading is reduced to 10cm. or below. There comes a time when the addition of another tablet will increase the reading. This is an indication that the dose is too strong. Generally the dose for Cuprum oxy. nig. plus Antimony crud. 1x works out at, say, two or three tablets, which I give three times a day. As the tablets have a some-what unpleasant taste, it may be better to give them after meals.

Parasites thrive in an acid condition of the intestines and, what-ever other treatment is given, I think it is good practice to include some anti-acid powder such as magnesium trisilicate or Bisodol, given in half a tumbler of water night and morning. An alternative to this is nitro-hydrochloric acid, which I have found to be very effective for the treatment of parasites.

To turn to an actual case, that of a man in his sixties who had had serious financial trouble and, so I was told, was not far off a nervous breakdown. It seemed he had lost interest in everything and I was asked if I could help. These were some of the readings I obtained:

General disease conditions		Rule readings	
			cm.
1. 80		Urea	70
2. 80		Uric acid	70
3. 70		Polarity	41–52/75
5. 80		Shock	70
10. 70		Septicaemia	75
		Anxiety neurosis	70
		Acidity	70
		Bone	48–80
	cm.	Parasites	80
Cancer toxins	70	Worms	80
Tumours, benign	80	Parasitic toxins	85
Tumours, malignant	75	Tape Worm	85
		Round worm	80

Lycopodium 30
Sulphur 30 } M.20. One of each n. and m.

Cuprum oxy. nig. plus Ant. crud. 1x. M.60. Two t.d.s., p.c.
Calbisnate. 1 drachm in half a tumbler of water n. and m.

This is a clear case of parasites with tape worm infection strongly indicated. There was acute general infection with what I call badly split polarity, i.e. where the readings for S and P, 52 and 75 respec-tively, are different. The first object in a case like this is to get rid of the parasites without bothering too much about specific virus and bacterial infections. The reading for cancer toxins and tumours should be taken as a measure of the gross toxaemia present and general disorganisation of the system. There must nevertheless have been a strong cancer diathesis in the condition. Lycopodium and Sulphur are both leading liver and bowel remedies and they cover a wide field of imbalance as shown by their symptomatology. They go well together and were doubtless tested on the *P* polarity reading of 75cm., bringing this down to under 10cm. Calbisnate was the proprietary anti-acid prescribed, very useful in such cases, whose manufacture has since been discontinued.

Ten days later the readings had improved somewhat, as the following table shows:

General disease conditions	Rule readings	cm.
1. 43	Shock	49
2. 43	Septicaemia	45
3. 42	Parasites	60
5. 44	Worms	72
6. 80	Tape worm	70
7. 80	Round worm	70
8. 80	Parasitic toxins	45
9. 69	Parasites, colon	80
10. 47	Liver	48–70
	Colon	48–75
	Stomach	50–60
	Cancer	47
	Cyst	75
	Tumour	80
	Sarcoma	80

Pulsatilla 1x
Podophyllum 1x } M.80. Take as directed.
Sabadilla 3x
Cuprum oxy. nig. plus Ant. crud. 1x. 12 tablets. Take as directed. Felix mas. 3 15-minim capsules.

These are the readings with prescription which I jotted down at the time. Often enough, where parasitic infection is not acute and one prefers to avoid using Cuprum oxy. nig., I have found the combination of the three remedies Pulsatilla, Podophyllum and Sabadilla very effective for dealing with worms. I use the first two remedies in the 1x potency and Sabadilla in the 3x potency. Ignatia 1x could be substituted for Podophyllum. Where it is more a case of prophylactic treatment or only a minor infection, I have used all three remedies in 3x potency. But naturally the 1x potencies are very much more effective in dealing with a fully developed live infection.

In the case under consideration, which I was convinced was one of tape worm, I decided to give drastic treatment with three 15-minim capsules of male fern, taken in conjunction with a short course of Cuprum oxy. nig. 1x tablets (twelve in all), followed by a course of the three remedies already mentioned. I was in close touch with the patient at the time and have no record of the exact procedure. But the results were significant. The patient had a severe purge and this treatment was undoubtedly the turning point in his recovery. He was instructed to take only a light diet and avoid at all costs alcohol and pig-meat in any shape or form. I knew that one glass of sherry or, for that matter, any sausage or bacon, would ruin the treatment instantly. I had read the riot act and my patient observed my instructions scrupulously.

This was a somewhat complicated case and several more treatments were required to get my patient back to normal. During this time I checked his endocrines, various organs and a number of rates relating to cancer and growths, and at one time used three Schüssler remedies in 6c potency, in addition to 3x remedies.

I should emphasise at this point that in all such work we are dealing with waveforms, and where a bad reaction for cancer, fibroma or tumour is obtained, this does not necessarily mean that the patient has any of these diseases. The great advantage of the radiesthetic method is that indications of a disease condition are obtained before, and sometimes long before, it has developed to the clinical stage. If a high reading for tumour is obtained and nothing is done, it is very probable that an actual tumour will eventually materialise. The patient in this case told me some little time after I had been treating him that he had a tape worm when a boy. It is doubtful if he ever got rid of the infection.

Where it is evident that parasitic infection has been present for some time, it may well be advisable to warn the patient against including pig-meat in his diet. Sausages can be a menace for such people and the patient will be wise to avoid them altogether, and for all time. The state of the bowels is an important factor in these cases, and some people, who are normally quite well in health, are very easily upset by consuming such things as boiled bacon, bacon rashers and sausages. Patients with a history of constipation should avoid pig-meat altogether.

It is very possible in my opinion that diverticulitis, or indeed the incidence of diverticulosis, can be associated with parasitic infection. It may be significant that while the Delawarr rate for parasitic toxins is 70088, that for diverticulitis is 40088. A positive reaction for the latter is a pointer for treatment, indicating an unhealthy condition of the bowel that should be attended to. It suggests a tendency for the patient to succumb to parasitic infection. It is often associated with catarrhal symptoms and Sabadilla, with or without Pulsatilla and Podophyllum, can prove useful in such cases.

As a prophylactic against the possibility of contracting parasitic infection, as from a salad taken in a restaurant, an anti-acid powder may be all that is necessary. The prescription for nitro-hydrochloric acid which I have used is also very effective. It is:

Acid Nitro-hydrochloric
mx. Aqua ad oz. 1
M. oz. 8.
1 teaspoonful in a little water t.d.s., p.c.

This prescription can be used double strength if required, i.e. mxx acid to oz. 1 water.

The way in which I came to diagnose one case of parasites was unusual. This was a child living overseas with her family. Her mother was under the impression that I had a specimen of her daughter and neglected to send me a new one. Some considerable time had elapsed since I treated this little girl. I had evidently thrown away the old specimen and it would have taken about a fortnight for me to write to her mother and for the mother to send me a new one and get the prescription back, bearing in mind the treble Air Mail journey necessary. However, her mother wroter her daughter's Christian name in capital letters in her letter to me and, after a minute or two's consideration, I cut the name out and placed it in a small vial. I then began testing, using the written name as a witness and thinking only of the girl.

At first nothing seemed to happen at all, and I was not sure whether in fact I was getting readings which meant anything. A number of disease conditions which I tested came out negative, and then I put up the rate for parasites or worms. My pendulum went right up the scale. So I prescribed for parasites. I heard later that the child improved immediately. There could be no doubt that the diagnosis was right as the prescription was specific for parasites and could not possibly have benefited the child if the trouble had been something else.

Where there is a real need, it is surprising sometimes what can be done through radiesthesia. If one sought to explain this sort of thing, one would probably not have the whole answer. At the psychic level it is possible for some radiesthetists to do without witnesses or specimens altogether, but for professional work I personally prefer to keep both feet as much as possible firmly on the ground.

Failure to diagnose parasites can be a serious matter. I offered to help a friend who had suffered from bad headaches and had at one time spent some days in a hospital for nervous diseases without receiving any real help. My diagnosis of worms was confirmed by a physiotherapist specialising in colonic irrigations and together we soon cleared the condition up—and the headaches. That unpleasant condition, itching of the anus, is often due to parasitic infection and may be so slight that it is difficult to diagnose. The combined rate of 80810851, i.e. parasites into rectum, may give the necessary clue, coming out slightly positive. Acute heartburn is sometimes due to the same cause. All that may be necessary for the cure of these conditions in a mild form is an anti-acid preparation.

Patients who contract parasitic infection easily may be subject at times to dizziness, sudden and urgent desire to urinate at night or in the early morning, and headaches. It may be difficult to say what the condition is and in subacute cases there may be little evidence of toxaemia on test. Nevertheless, in such a patient, an unhealthy intestinal tract is almost an axiom, and considerable benefit may be derived from a course of such remedies as Pulsatilla, Ignatia, Podophyllum and Sabadilla in 3x potency, say two tablets of each t.d.s.

Radiesthesia can sometimes help to explain the symptomatology of a drug. Podophyllum has the symptoms of diarrhoea, especially in the morning, 'green, watery, fetid, profuse, gushing' (Boericke). I had a patient with very much these symptoms and found she was suffering from parasites. It is not surprising that Podophyllum is a good remedy on test for parasites.

Growths

A great advantage of the homoeopathic remedy is its dispersive character. In it there is a dynamic force which acts on any matter or tissue with which it syntonises. It is thus a great eliminator, its action being from within outwards or, if you like, from the centre to the periphery. A suitable drug in medium to high potency will disintegrate a virus if the potency of the drug is matched to the activation, or virulence, of the virus. When dealing with diseased or compacted tissue, low potencies acting at the tissue level, and nearer by comparison to crude chemical drugs, will act directly on the affected organ or tissue and greatly add to whatever curative power higher potencies can provide. In deep-seated disease a high-potency remedy may be required to change the direction of the vital forces within the body away from disease to health. But it may well be that low potency remedies will decide whether, for instance, a fibroma can be destroyed. The higher potencies will deal with whatever virus or bacterial infections are present and initiate the elimination of toxins, but low potency remedies may still be required to restore diseased or compacted tissue to a normal state of health and function.

It must be repeated therefore that an advantage of the homoeopathic remedy is that we can treat disease at different levels and apply suitable potencies to disperse, or eradicate, the agents of disease at the opposite ends of the scale—at the upper end where we have the microscopic virus or bacterium in a high degree of activation, and at the lower end where we are dealing with tissue that may be grossly diseased.

Even so, it must be pointed out that when using low potencies such as 3x, the remedy has a heightened power of dispersal through the fact that it is potentised. Being also of a dilution of 1 in 1,000, any toxic propensities that it may have are far less than those of crude drugs. Nevertheless, by the fact that it is potentised, its action can be far more effective, as for example in toning up an organ such as the stomach or liver.

In dealing with a gross condition such as a fibroma or tumour, it may be advisable to use a remedy of a potency even lower than 3x. I should say that a 1x potency is very nearly equivalent in action to a crude non-potentised drug, but it may be less toxic, having a dilution of 1 in 10. In my experience one should seldom, if ever, need to go below the 1x potency when using homoeopathic remedies. It is possible to employ some of these in mother tincture, or undiluted, form. On test I have found such tinctures to be contraindicated, except perhaps for the first few doses.

We have seen how 1x drugs can be wanted in dealing with parasites, a truly gross condition. I have often thought how much better medication by orthodox methods would be if orthodox drugs, i.e. those used in allopathy, were prepared in 1x potency. Even in such a potency there must be some dispersive action, even if of very slight proportions, which adds to the effectiveness of the drug, which meanwhile is less toxic than crude drugs. As a radiesthetist I venture it as my opinion that crude drugs are unnecessarily strong in their action on human tissue. As it is, there are many highly skilled homoeopaths who seldom use potencies below, say, 6c or even 30c. But to return to tumours and growths.

Supposing that we have to deal with that not uncommon complaint, a uterine fibroma. Knowing that we must treat the patient as a whole, we will test for any pathogenic organisms present in the system and check organs, endocrines, etc., as considered necessary. We shall then find that certain remedies are required in, say, the 6, 12 or 30c potency to deal with the pathogens. Next we will put up the rate for uterine fibroma and find two or more 3x remedies which will cut out its waveform. We would naturally want to test remedies which are known to deal with this condition. For this we could consult a repertory.

A friend woke up early one morning with excruciating pain in the uterine area. The pain was so bad that her husband rang up the doctor, who hurried to her bedside and gave her an injection to stop the pain. Later my friend and I both thought it would be a good idea to see what the pendulum could tell us. These are readings I jotted down at the time, obtained on the rule:

General disease conditions

1. 43		Depression	70
2. 44		Anxiety neurosis	70
3. 43		Shock	56
5. 42		Trauma (injury)	56
6. 45		Parasites	53
7. 52		Septicaemia	55
8. 40		Bone	49–55
9. 47		Subluxation	70
10. 68		Vertebral joints	50–50
		Ilio-sacral joints	50–55
		Tuberculosis	75
		T.B. Bovinum	70
		T.B. Bovinum, uterus	75
		Uterine fibroma	60
		Cyst	65
		Cyst, ovarian	65
		Ovaries	50–65
		Uterus	52/55–70

Lycopus vir. 6 M.60. One t.d.s., a.c.

Causticum 3x ⎫
Pulsatilla 3x ⎭ M.40. Two of each b.d., a.c.

I thought it might be a good idea to give this patient some direct microsonic treatment by means of a Delawarr instrument, as well as treatment with remedies. I note that I treated her for T.B., but have no record of the rate used. In all probability I put the complementary rate for T.B. into the uterus, which is the conventional way of saying that I put up the anti-T.B. rate, 608, followed by that for uterus. I may also have treated directly the uterine fibroma. In the event I only gave my friend one treatment, but in the middle of it she said she felt something 'give' in the area under treatment. It was not unpleasant and she was rather pleased about it. Whatever my treatment did, or did not do for her, she had no return of the trouble.

Although there was undoubtedly a diathesis towards uterine fibroma, nothing of the kind had necessarily manifested itself on

the physical plane. It is accepted in radionic circles that the waveform of a disease generally shows up on test before there is any
clinical evidence of such a condition. The dynamic pattern of the
disease is formed, to be followed later by the physical disease.
Pulsatilla is one of the most useful remedies we have for dealing with
T.B. So is Lycopus vir. In this case Causticum 3x and Pulsatilla 3x,
both singly and together, cut out the waveforms of both T.B. and
uterine fibroma. My friend had domestic worries and was suffering
from depression. This accounts for the high reading obtained on the
rate for depression.

In another case I had, the patient had had a hysterectomy, but
the rates for fibroid and uterine fibroma still gave a high reading
and reactions for T.B. were also obtained. The reason why one can
obtain a positive reading for uterine fibroma in such a case is probably because there is still tissue in the patient having the uterine
waveform, just as it is possible to obtain readings for the appendix
in a case who has undergone an appendectomy. This patient was
treated with Pulsatilla, which cleared up the T.B. reactions and very
much reduced the readings for fibroma. Lapis albus in low potency
is often valuable for the treatment of tumours and fibromas. Silica
is another remedy which should be tested.

Meningococcus

This is the case of a girl of nine who was shortly to undertake a
long sea voyage with her family from a South African port. Her
mother told me that the child was extremely restless, over-energetic,
and suffered from insomnia. She had had a cold and cough and
seemed to have some difficulty in breathing. Sometimes she woke
at midnight and could not sleep again. The mother did not want to
give the child a sedative or anything non-homoeopathic.

General disease conditions	Rule readings	
		cm.
1. 40	Septicaemia	40
2. 45	Parasitic infection	44
3. 43	Brain	49–50
5. 45	Spinal cord	50–65
	Bone	50–50
Urea 55cm.	Meningitis	65
Uric acid 55cm.	T.B. Meningitis	67

The readings I recorded are given above. The General Disease
Conditions were all negative, from which I would deduce that the
mother had been trying to help the child on her own account. At

the same time Urea and Uric acid were both positive—55, so it was obvious that active infection was present. The readings for inflammation of brain, spinal cord and bone are all positive, that for spinal cord being especially bad.

The most significant readings on rates were those for Meningococcus and T.B. Meningitis, which were well up the scale at 65 and 67cm. respectively. I also tested with the nosodes, probably on the *P* polarity reading as well as affected organs. Latyrus 6 was the indicated remedy, but I wanted to find a 3x remedy which the mother could give her daughter at any time to quieten her down and help her to sleep. Gelsemium, which is an excellent remedy for inflammatory conditions where the nervous system is affected, proved on test to meet my requirements. So I posted my Air Mail letter off with instructions without delay. The prescription was:

Latyrus 6 M.40. 1 b.d. for 17 days.
Gelsemium 3x. M.100. 2 t.d.s. for 17 days, or as directed.

Whether or not the mother found it necessary to give the complete course of Gelsemium 3x, I felt this was a useful remedy for her to have by her for future eventualities. She was an experienced homoeopath and knew when to cut down treatment. In the event the child responded very quickly.

This was, of course, a straightforward case, very different from a highly toxic one in which one can sometimes get all kinds of positive readings, which can so often only be resolved gradually by a sequence of prescriptions. The mother wrote just before the family sailed that her daughter had shown a tremendous improvement, 'In fact we were staggered last night when she asked to go to bed! Just after 8 p.m.! I can't tell you how grateful I am.'

This was one of those cases which gives one renewed faith in the radiesthetic method. This lady and I had been corresponding intermittently for years, but had never met. Nevertheless, I think we would both claim that we had established an understanding and friendship between us—thanks to radiesthesia!

Haemorrhoids

Haemorrhoids are a painful, if common, complaint. If they disappear promptly following treatment, the effectiveness of the treatment is clear. It is not just a case of the patient feeling better!

One way of dealing with an attack is to set the rate for haemorrhoids on the instrument, and with the rule-cum-vial connection arrangement, place nosodes in turn alongside the vial at 100cm. It is quite probable that the reading for haemorrhoids will be only slightly positive, say 47 or 50cm. This leaves ample room on the scale for getting positive readings with the nosodes. There is always the alternative method available whereby the nosodes can be placed in turn alongside the specimen at 0cm.

The sort of factors present in the attack will be bacterial infections such as B. coli, B. typhosus coli, Streptococcus and Staphylococcus. With nosodes alongside the 100cm. mark, likely remedies for specific infections can be tested by placing them alongside the specimen at 0cm. Any remedy which reduces the reading to below 10cm. is a good remedy to deal with the infection under test. Final choice of remedies can be made on the P polarity.

Tests for infection could, of course, be equally well made on the triangle and suitable remedies chosen. One check that could be made would be by testing the remedies on the witness for rectum. In a bad case, with the rectum giving a very bad reading, 3x remedies could be tested to tone up the rectum in addition to the higher potency remedies dealing with any infections present. Aesculus hip., Ruta, Podophyllum, Lycopodium, Carbo veg, Ignatia, Nux vomica, Collinsonia and Causticum are some of the remedies which might suit. Silica is excellent where indicated and Arnica can be useful for reducing toxins—and pain! Some of these remedies act on the liver, which almost invariably needs treatment in such cases. A combination of remedies which has been found to be useful is Podophyllum and Ruta, while some cases may do better with Lycopodium and Nux vomica, perhaps with the addition of Carbo veg. or Causticum. In the 6c potency (or higher), Sulphur or Sepia can be invaluable.

I think it will generally be found that people addicted to haemorrhoids have some kind of weakness in the spine. This may be a subluxation. If the sacro-iliac joint is affected, it may be advisable to find out by X-ray (with the patient standing equally on both feet) whether one leg is longer than the other. If this is so, a heel cushion fixed in the appropriate shoe may put the matter right. Chronic cases of haemorrhoids can derive, as I believe, from deformity, to whatever extent, of the lower spine.

Debility

All too frequently a patient complains of debility, when there appears to be nothing very much wrong. More often than not this debility is due to a toxic condition arising from current or past infections. Tests with nosodes, rates or witnesses will often indicate what the cause, or causes, are. It may be a case of residual toxins derived from past infections, metal poisoning, faecal poisons, and so on. Any disease, or disease condition, giving a positive reading must, of course, be treated.

Generally remedies in 6c or 30c potency will be chosen. If it is a subacute case with a normal polarity and a ncar-normal reading for urea and uric acid, 6c remedies will generally be required. These will be required over a period to reduce general toxaemia as well as deal with virus or microbial infection, whereas higher potencies might be required in a really acute attack of infection in which the system was badly disorganised. But in addition to the 6c remedies, improvement will often be accelerated and the patient made to feel much more comfortable, if 3x remedies are prescribed at the same time. These act directly on the affected tissues and accelerate the elimination of toxins. Rightly prescribed, they will also tone up nerves and organs.

Knowing the patient, the practitioner will have a better idea of the remedies required and on what they should be tested. If a patient has had abdominal operations, his intestines may be his weak point. Remedies can then be usefully tested on these organs. Or they may be tested on the rate for toxins. Simple tests on the P polarity reading may be all that is required in a straightforward case. It is naturally desirable that remedies chosen should deal effectively with any general disease conditions present, such as active virus or microbial infection.

People suffering from weakness and debility will sometimes give a bad bone reading. When this happens their nerves invariably suffer. Appropriate remedies should deal with such conditions as 'inflammation' or 'deficiency' of bone. Bone remedies such as Arnica, Causticum, Lycopodium and Silica in 3x potency will sometimes help a patient to regain his normal level of vitality and well-being in a very short space of time. They can also be useful for getting rid of toxins and toning up the system generally. We might claim that homoeopathic Nux vomica is the nearest equivalent to the proprietary tonic medicine which people purchase at their chemist, and Nux vomica 3x is always a great help when it is needed and correctly indicated. Arnica and Silica, Causticum and Silica, Nux vomica and Silica, Nux vomica and Lycopodium—these are the kind of combinations which have proved their worth. Where Nux vomica is definitely needed, it will measure up very well on bone, although not a bone remedy. Any remedy which a patient really needs will measure up quite well on any disease condition as represented by a rate, even if it does not reduce the reading to below 10cm.

If the digestive system is at fault, Carbo veg. and Nux vomica, which go very well together, should be considered, perhaps with the addition of Lycopodium. Kali bich. may be found good for a duodenal case. A case of indigestion showing typhoid reactions may well benefit from Arsenic alb., Baptisia or Bryonia. In a prolonged case of debility and general malaise, it may be a good thing to consider and test for the Schüssler salts.

I might mention that Dr. Richards, who used to employ sometimes as many as eight remedies in the 6 or 30 potency, almost invariably accompanied them with two or three remedies in the 3x potency. These were chosen from the remedies in the higher potency and I can testify to the success of this method. There may come a time when the patient realises that he has had enough of the higher potency remedies before the prescription is finished. Often enough in such cases he can continue with the 3x remedies quite happily and these will often clear up residual toxins, tone up the digestive organs and nerves and make the patient feel considerably better than he otherwise would.

Eight remedies in the 6c or 30c potency prescribed together are of course rather many, and I think it would be generally agreed today, bearing in mind the advances that have been made in methods of radiesthetic testing, that more than two or three remedies in either of these potencies should seldom be found necessary.

Blood pressure

It may surprise some people that we can put up rates on a radionic instrument for blood pressure. Rates are given by the Delawarr Laboratories for high, low and normal blood pressure, these being 409046, 4090768 and 4090734 respectively. For testing high and low blood pressure, we would put the first dial at 40, as these are disease conditions. Normal blood pressure is not a disease condition, but presumably it is intended that the first dial should be used when putting up this rate also. Readings thus obtained could be compared with those obtained on the rule by leaving the first dial at 0 and putting up the first digit 4 on the second dial, 0 on the third, and so on. When using the vial connection, I doubt if there is any point in using the rate for normal blood pressure.

One can only expect to obtain a general indication of what the blood pressure is by using the rates for H.B.P. and L.B.P., but where the blood pressure cannot be taken manually, this can be useful. If the rate for H.B.P. gives a reading higher than that for L.B.P., we should expect the blood pressure to be above normal for the patient under test. Conversely, with L.B.P. showing a higher reading than H.B.P., we assume that the blood pressure is on the low side. A check on the rate for suprarenal gland, and on the state of the endocrine glands generally, may help to confirm the diagnosis.

Normal readings for H.B.P. and L.B.P. would be 45cm. But if the patient is in a toxic condition and disease conditions generally give positive readings, we may get a reading of 50, 55 or 60cm. for H.B.P. and L.B.P. If the two readings are the same, blood pressure may be near normal. It is the *difference* between the two readings which will tell us whether the blood pressure is on the high or low side.

If remedies are given to the patient showing high readings for both H.B.P. and L.B.P., these should reduce both readings to 45cm. We know that as one disease condition is treated and its reading on the scale is reduced, readings for other disease conditions will also be reduced—to whatever extent. As treatment proceeds and the readings for disease conditions are reduced, they will often fall below 45cm.

If a patient consults a practitioner and both readings (for high and low B.P.) are found to be, say, 40cm., it is safe to conclude that the patient has been receiving treatment. He may well have been treating himself, as those interested in homoeopathy so often do. It is possible that his system has been over-stimulated by remedies to some extent. Further treatment should bring the two readings up to 45cm.

Diet

It was an American who produced for my inspection a bottle of wheat extract, marketed in the United States. Claimed to have valuable therapeutic properties, it was more in the nature of a concentrated food than a medicament. I tested it out on the rule and came to the conclusion that it had some excellent properties. The sort of test I made was to find its effect on the reading for debility, when it took the pendulum right down the rule.

This American was having homoeopathic treatment at the time and despite the fact that his liver should have been in perfect order, on test it proved to be definitely toxic. So I wondered if he was taking too much of the wheat extract. I tested for dosage in the following way.

I put a small vial of the extract on the triangle at B, and *P* (acetylcholine) at C. With my visitor's specimen at A the pendulum balanced along CD, showing that it suited him. I then placed an empty vial at B and poured in a drop of the extract at a time, meanwhile allowing the pendulum to oscillate along CD. As the tenth drop entered the vial, the pendulum swung off to the right, balancing at about 10°. Further drops increased the reading. I concluded that the correct dose was ten drops (exactly as far as my memory serves), although on the bottle it was given as one tablespoonful twice a day. Too much of a highly concentrated food will poison the system, and this is what was happening to my visitor!

Placing any aliment or liquid intended for consumption at B

with the human specimen at A, and P at C, is a good way of finding out whether the item tested agrees with the subject. If it does, the pendulum should balance along CD. S (liquid adrenalin) instead of P could equally well be placed at C. Alternatively the food or drink could be tested on the sympathetic and parasympathetic nervous systems, S and P being successively placed at B with the aliment just outside the circle. Anything which suits would balance the pendulum along CD.

I had a patient who told me that onions were the one thing which disagreed with her. So I decided to test her for onions on the rule and triangle. On the triangle with her specimen alone at A, the pendulum balanced at 0° (or along CD). My sample of boiled onions placed at A, with nothing else on the triangle, gave the same reading. Then with her specimen at A and the onion sample at B and with P at C, the pendulum swung round to 50°, which was also the reading I obtained by replacing P by S. This was a very bad reading and confirmed what I had been told about onions not agreeing with my patient.

Her sympathetic and parasympathetic nervous systems, represented by S and P respectively placed in turn at B, each gave a reading of 30°. Bringing the onion sample up in turn alongside S and P, but just outside the circle, increased the reading to 40° tested on S and to 50° tested on P. I next decided to test this patient on the P polarity on the rule. The onion sample reduced her P polarity reading of 38cm. to only 32cm. If it had been really good for her it would have reduced the reading to 15cm. or less. This is an easy and useful precision test for finding whether any food or drink, or for that matter any medicine potentised or unpotentised, is suitable for the person under test. I might add that the onion sample had a polarity of 40–40/40, so it was a perfectly good sample. This could also be deduced by the fact that placed alone at A on the triangle, the pendulum balanced along CD.

It may happen that whereas an aliment suits a patient generally, it may have a harmful effect on a particular organ. It is obvious that in a case of duodenal ulcer, for example, the aliment should be tested on it. In a similar manner, if a patient with a bad heart indulges in some kind of alcohol, this should be tested on the heart in addition to any general test, such as that on the P polarity. It hardly needs to be said that tobacco is extremely bad for both these conditions.

Let us take the specimen of a young man presumably in reasonably good health and find what effect tobacco and aluminium have on his heart, duodenum and lungs. Using the triangle, the results were:

	degrees
Heart	20
Heart, plus tobacco	30
Heart, plus aluminium	25
Heart, plus tobacco and aluminium	30
Lungs	30
Lungs, plus tobacco	40
Lungs, plus aluminium	35
Lungs, plus tobacco and aluminium	40
Duodenum	0
Duodenum, plus tobacco	30
Duodenum, plus aluminium	10
Duodenum, plus tobacco and aluminium	30

While neither the heart nor lungs give good readings, that for duodenum is normal. Tobacco is obviously more of a poison to the subject than aluminium and it affects all three organs equally. Let us now find what effect, if any, tobacco and aluminium have on any tendency to cancer. For this we put up a witness of Carcinoma at B. The readings were:

	degrees
Carcinoma	20
Carcinoma, plus tobacco	30
Carcinoma, plus aluminium	20
Carcinoma, plus tobacco and aluminium	30

In each case the tobacco or aluminium was placed at B just outside the circle. The reading of 20° for Carcinoma may be taken as normal, but if the subject had a cancer diathesis, it is obvious that tobacco would augment it. The effect of aluminium is apparently nil. Nevertheless, as I believe, aluminium can be extremely damaging to any unhealthy tissue and it might be expected to worsen any actual case of clinical cancer. Some people are allergic to aluminium and others are not. But in acute disease I suspect that cooking the patient's food in an aluminium container or boiling water in an aluminium kettle could only aggravate the case. Aluminium appears to have the unpleasant characteristic of attacking a person at his weakest spot. This may explain why the symptoms of aluminium poisoning can be so varied.

The human specimen under examination gave a normal P polarity reading of 38. Tested on it tobacco gave a reading of 32 and aluminium one of 25. This confirms that tobacco was more of a poison than aluminium for the specimen's owner.

At one time I was gratified to find that for myself Dubonnet produced a reading of about 5cm. on the *P* polarity test, as it is a drink I very much like and it always seemed to agree with me. I was not altogether surprised to find that Phospherine tablets were equally well indicated, as each contains quinine. This was probably not unconnected with the fact that at the time I was obtaining reactions for malaria.

Poliomyelitis

A correspondent suspected he was suffering from a hernia or another complaint he mentioned, and wrote to me and asked if I could check him up radiesthetically. He told me at the same time that he was having treatment from a biochemist in whom he had every confidence. Using his letter as a sample, I told him that the rate for hernia gave a positive reading. The other complaint, if it existed, was passive, for it gave no positive indications. I also told him that the investigation he wanted was really one for a surgeon.

It was quite some time later that I heard from this correspondent again, asking to come and see me. He told me I was right about the hernia and he had been operated on for it. He had a strap on his right foot, as the muscles of his foot gave out following an attack of sciatica some months previously. He complained of general debility, had a poor physique and was obviously of a highly nervous disposition. He had just retired from business and the hoped-for improvement in his health had not taken place. He had been having biochemic treatment over a long period of time.

I asked this patient to lie on my couch face downwards and went over his spine with my pendulum. I obtained strong negative reactions all along his spine, which were especially bad in the upper dorsal region. I obtained slight reactions for typhoid and para-typhoid and a bad reaction for poliomyelitis, which gave a reading of 65cm. on the rule with vial connection to radionic instrument. Bone radiation was poor, giving a reading of 46cm. with the rate 0·84 set on the instrument. Bone did not show inflammation, but 'lack of tone'. The liver and organs generally were below average and vitality was obviously low.

I prescribed Gelsemium 6, 1 t.d.s., a.c., and Lycopodium 3x and Nux vomica 3x, 2 tablets of each t.d.s., a.c. The prescription was to last three weeks, but my patient rang me up after about a fortnight to say he was feeling much better and I told him to reduce dosage. Meanwhile a second appointment was made.

The patient looked quite different when I saw him again. There was colour in his cheeks and he was quite sprightly compared with when I first saw him. He said he felt quite different. He was not wearing the strap on his foot. He explained to me that as he walked his foot had a tendency to slap down on the ground, but he seemed to manage very well without the strap. I went over his spine again with my pendulum and was surprised to find how his back had improved. The pendulum gyrated anti-clockwise very slowly in small circles along his spine, so slowly in fact that I could find no really bad spots anywhere.

He complained of sudden urges to urinate and asked me to check his bladder. On the triangle the pendulum showed inflammation by oscillating to the left of the line CD (see diagram on page 33). As I have explained, in testing organs on the triangle we usually obtain a reading to the right of the line CD, usually of 10° or more. If we call these readings negative, showing lack of function, an active but inflamed organ will often give a positive reading of 10° or more to the left of the line CD.

My test of the bladder for inflammation on the rule produced a positive reading of about 55cm. Using nosodes placed in radiative contact with the patient's specimen at 0cm., I diagnosed a B. coli infection of the bladder. This was confirmed by putting up the rate for B. coli into bladder, i.e. 301762. There was also some indication of catarrh of the bladder and I found that Causticum 6 and Ipecac. 6 corrected the condition and measured up well on the P polarity. I prescribed these two remedies to be taken t.d.s. for a fortnight.

This was a straightforward case and the response of the patient was excellent. I suggested that he should take up exercises on the Harriet Nyemann method to strengthen his general muscular system and, in particular, the muscles of his right foot. The conclusion I came to was that this patient must have contracted at some time a mild attack of poliomyelitis and had never got rid of the toxins.

Chapter 10

Radionics

So far I have only made passing reference to the orthodox techniques employed in radionics. For diagnosing by the stick method, using a radionic diagnostic instrument, an exact routine is laid down by the Delawarr Laboratories, which was outlined in *I.M.R.R.* The practice of radionics also includes treatment by the broadcasting method, colour therapy, and by direct microsonic therapy. In the latter case the patient sits in front of a radionic instrument, which generates sonic radiation. The instrument may be a broadcast instrument designed also for sonic therapy, or it may be designed solely for microsonic treatment. In either case rates are set on the instrument panel in exactly the same way as for broadcasting.

As I am not concerned in this book with orthodox radionic techniques, I shall only make passing reference to radionic broadcasting and direct microsonic treatment. In any case my experience of them is limited. But as one reads from time to time statements about radionic broadcasting, which would appear to suggest that any therapeutic effect is primarily of a mental character—that the one important factor is what is in the mind of the operator and that it matters little what rates are set on the instrument—a word or two about my own experiences may not be out of place.

The first case I had which convinced me of what can be achieved by accurate diagnosis and correct assessment of the rate, or rates, to be employed, was of a Jamaican who suffered acutely from psoriasis. He was an engineer employed by one of the big oil companies, and when in Britain had been in the care of one of London's teaching hospitals. He had had his nails removed twice and had tried various treatments, all without effect. On a second visit to Britain he got in touch with me. I mentioned this case in *I.M.R.R.* and how I came to treat him by broadcast with the complementary rate for ringworm, despite the fact that orthodox tests had come out negative for this condition. While he was in this country I mostly treated this patient with homoeopathic remedies and, when he visited me, with direct microsonic treatment. Part of the time he was up north, and on several occasions when the condition worsened, he wrote to let me know and I then treated him by broadcast with the complementary rate for ringworm. In every case he improved considerably. When the time came for his return to Jamaica, my patient was convinced that he had found an answer to his problem. The psoriasis had almost disappeared and he was duly elated. But unfortunately, when he got back to Jamaica, he had a severe setback. Undoubtedly the climate was largely to blame. If he had stayed in this country it is very probable that, with the minimum of treatment, he would have been able to live quite comfortably. But the point I wish to make is that there was one rate which did help this intractable case very considerably. No other rate which I tried had any noticeable effect. This was all a long time ago and I have learnt much since those days.

It was when dealing with this case that I discovered that the broadcast instrument when earthed, as is required for broadcasting, was upsetting my nervous system. I think anyone with a history of spinal trouble could be equally affected. As my work at this time was to some extent experimental, I spent considerable periods of time standing over the instrument testing out different rates. Moreover the room where I was working was a very small one. I think it is just as well that all radionic practitioners should realise that there is a possible danger for themselves, or those around them, if they are working with broadcast instruments connected to earth for considerable periods of time. At the same time I believe it is claimed that some broadcast instruments, which do not incorporate a magnet in their design, cannot have this sort of effect.

It was partly because of this susceptibility to such effects, which I know exist in other people, that I have done little broadcasting work myself and have mostly restricted myself to homoeopathy, with occasional direct microsonic treatments and broadcast treatment reserved for special cases, and for emergencies. The relative advantages or disadvantages of the different methods employed could be argued *ad nauseam*, but in the end the practitioner must decide for himself what method, or methods, he will use. A possible disadvantage of broadcasting is that close supervision is necessary all the time the instruments are in use and, contrary to some others, I am of the opinion that the length of broadcast treatment can be an important factor in a case. The effectiveness of broadcast treatment cannot be denied by those who have studied it and experimented with it. I occasionally treat myself by broadcast for short periods and on one or two occasions the results have surprised me.

For reasons which I need not go into, I have been subject much of my life to periods of acute nervous debility. On one occasion I felt so ill that for some two months I had to spend a good deal of the time on my back. To walk about was a distinct effort and I had the feeling that I might collapse at any moment. My legs felt like sticks and it was quite an adventure to walk out of the house! As can happen when the nervous system is badly depleted, I could get no positive reactions for infection. Truth to tell I felt so ill that I had given up trying and an orthodox medical examination revealed nothing that was wrong.

And then, one day, I went into my study and started making one or two tests. I put up the general rate for tuberculosis and obtained a slight positive reaction. Then I added the rate for bone and the pendulum went right up the scale. So I treated myself by broadcast with the complementary rate for T.B. into bone. Nothing very much happened. But when I woke the next morning I suddenly decided I wanted to go to London. This I did and had one of the best days I have ever had in town.

On a later occasion my nervous system again went to pieces and I again obtained bad reactions for T.B. Putting the general rate for T.B. (402) into various organs, I found that many were affected. I found I could clear the infection in an organ by broadcast by putting up the anti-T.B. rate, i.e. the complementary rate of 402, which is 608, into the organ, but soon realised that it was extremely doubtful whether I could clear my whole system by treating each organ in turn. Something else was required.

I decided that a strong T.B. remedy was needed that could be put on the instrument and used in conjunction with the anti-T.B. rate. Through my tests I had come to the conclusion that Pulsatilla was one of the best T.B. remedies we have and, with testing on the rule, Pulsatilla 1x cut out the reading for T.B. completely, bringing it right down the scale. The result was that I quickly cleared my system of this infection and my nervous system returned to normal.

Readings for tuberculosis may refer to an actual T.B. infection or to T.B. toxins, which could well be hereditary. Such infections have a habit of boiling up in much the same way as an old malarial infection does. A course of treatment with Pulsatilla 1x tablets, given in conjunction with whatever other remedies are necessary, and perhaps including Pulsatilla in some higher potency also, should clear a subacute case up once and for all. Specific tests, previously described, to find the exact number of Pulsatilla 1x tablets to a dose, should be made, the prescription being three doses a day.

I remember once, when I was getting T.B. reactions for myself, I obtained a high reading for T.B. in the colon. When I treated this by broadcast with the anti-T.B. rate into the colon, I had the sensation of my inside being lifted up. The reaction was so strong that the tension of the abdominal muscles was too great to be comfortable. Nevertheless it was a very pleasant sensation, a great improvement to anything that could be achieved by wearing a belt! To react so strongly is unusual, but it was due to several operations I had had in this region in the past. But it did convince me, as nothing else could, of the value and validity of broadcast treatment and the importance of putting up the correct rates.

In making an examination in which the diagnosis is doubtful, it is always advisable to add the rate for an organ to that for a disease condition. The general T.B. rate 402 may give a reading of little more than 45cm. But if we add the rate for lungs, small intestine, bone, or any other organ which is suspect, the reading may go up the scale to 55cm. or more. Supposing we are testing a case of erysipelas. The reading may quite easily be 45cm., or thereabouts. But if we add the rate for skin, a higher reading may be obtained. An infection is often only active in one particular organ, although through radiesthesia it may be found to exist in other parts of the system also.

In a mild case of T.B., the *general* rate may give a negative reading, especially if treatment for the condition has already been given, but specific rates for the disease such as 4031, 6088 or 8086 (the bovine type) may show up positive. This is understandable. An organ may appear to be normal on test, but if we add it to the general rate for bacterial infection or toxins, a positive reading may be obtained. Treatment by broadcast of the organs of the alimentary tract by putting up the general treatment rate for bacterial infection or toxins, followed in turn by the rates for the various organs, may make a patient feel considerably better. And incidentally the four-figure rate for toxins of 6065 provided by Dr. Ruth Drown may be useful in such cases, this rate being used for both diagnosis and treatment, according to Drown practice.

Rates for diagnosing a disease condition are known as recognition rates. According to the Delawarr Laboratories the treatment rates, i.e. the rates used for radionic broadcasting, should be the complementary rates. The recognition rate for Streptococcus pyogenes is 6057. The complementary rate for this is 4053. This is obtained by subracting the figure 60 on the first dial (used for disease conditions) from 100 and the figures on subsequent dials from 10. The complementary rate of 0 is taken as 0 and that of 50 is taken as 90. 50 is the rate for cancer and the idea of using 90 as the complementary rate is to avoid broadcasting an actual cancer rate.

The truth is that a disease condition can be treated with either the recognition or treatment rates. In the Delawarr book of rates the rate for S. typhi is given as 2014, while that for epidemic typhoid is 8096, which is the complement of 2014. The rates are obviously closely analogous. Practitioners using Drown instruments employ recognition rates as treatment rates, and it may be that for the treatment of virus and bacterial infections, recognition rates may sometimes be more effective than their complementary rates. But when using recognition rates the time of treatment is in my opinion far more important and could be critical. There would seem to be no reason why both recognition and complementary rates are not used during a treatment. The validity of the complementary rate is further discussed in Chapter 16.

As some practitioners are much more skilful with the pendulum than with the stick method of testing in conjunction with a radionic instrument, a few words may not be out of place on the technique of broadcasting with the assistance of a pendulum. Let us consider the wall type of Delawarr broadcast instrument, which has one metal plate on top together with a tuning dial to operate the internal magnet. No aerial is provided.

First we set the nine dials for setting up the rates at 0 and connect the instrument to earth. Then we turn the tuning dial to 1, which is at 12 o'clock on the tuning dial face as we stand in front of the instrument. It will be found that with that setting of the tuning dial, the pendulum does not gyrate when held over the metal plate. Indeed we might say that it is inert. The specimen of the patient is put on the plate and orientated, i.e. it is turned slowly round in a clockwise direction until the pendulum held over it gyrates clockwise strongly. Next we set up the rate required for treatment and, with the pendulum held this time over the tuning dial, we turn the dial slowly clockwise until we obtain a gyration. If the practitioner has a portable detector, this could be attached to the instrument and the pendulum held over it for tuning. It would be best to use the detector without a rubber pad as is needed for obtaining a stick.

To get good results in broadcasting, it is important that the tuning dial is accurately set. It can be checked in the following way. Supposing we are treating a patient for a B. coli infection of the bladder, with the complementary rate for B. coli into the bladder (709362) set on the instrument. We can now put up the recognition rate for B. coli into bladder (301762) on another instrument connected to the rule by means of the vial connection, with another specimen of the patient at 0cm. If the broadcast instrument is correctly tuned, we will get a balance point of 10cm., or under. If it is, say, 15cm., we can turn the tuning dial of the broadcast instrument slightly, in one direction or the other, until the reading is brought down to under 10cm.

If we have not got a second instrument, with only the patient's specimen on the rule, we should be able to obtain a reading of 100cm., if the instrument in use is correctly tuned. As treatment proceeds, the reading will gradually fall. When it has reached about 50cm., that may be a good time to stop treatment. If it is required to employ a remedy for distant treatment in addition to whatever rate is chosen, this could be orientated at one end of the metal plate on the broadcast instrument with the patient's specimen at the other end. As an alternative a remedy could presumably be placed on the portable detector plate and orientated by pendulum.

When employing direct microsonic treatment with the patient sitting in front of the microsonic instrument, it is desirable that the treatment should be checked on the rule with the patient's specimen at 0cm. and a vial-cum-instrument arrangement at the other end of the rule. If it is more convenient, the rule may be in a room separate from the treatment room.

With the recognition rate of the condition treated set on the instrument, it will be found that as treatment proceeds, the rule balance point gradually moves down the scale. When it has reached under 10cm., that is the time to stop treatment. The waveform of the condition being treated has been at least temporarily destroyed. If we are dealing with a gross condition such as a tumour, we must anticipate that the waveform of the condition will return, perhaps again giving a positive reading on the rule. In this case repetitive microsonic treatments will be required. In microsonic treatment I think it is generally agreed that complementary rates for disease conditions only should be used.

Chapter 11

Nuclear Fall-Out

The medical authorities have been much concerned over the damage to health from nuclear fall-out as a result of experimental nuclear bomb testing. Four elements released by fall-out which are especially dangerous to health are strontium, caesium, iodine and carbon. It is the radioactive isotope of strontium, Strontium 90, which has a predilection for bone. Yttrium is a daughter product of strontium and may be similarly implicated. Strontium is found largely in vegetables and bread, also in milk. It may produce bone tumours and anaemia. Radioactive iodine is found in milk and is especially dangerous to children, as it has an affinity for the thyroid gland and can easily constitute a strong dose to the small thyroid of a child. It can cause cancer of the thyroid.

Radioactive caesium and Carbon 14 comprise genetic risks, and while they come in very small doses, they nevertheless persist for very long periods. Sterility can be caused in both the male and female by excessive radiation. Radium, strontium and other radioactive elements are accumulated by, and retained in, bone. Experience has shown that the employment of X-rays for both diagnosis and treatment can be dangerous to health.

Strontium 90 is absorbed by bone in a similar manner to calcium. Due to nuclear tests the ratio of Strontium 90 to calcium in the bones of young children doubled in 1963 compared with 1962, according to a report of the Medical Research Committee published in November, 1964. This agreed with an earlier report by the Agricultural Research Council that the ratio of Strontium 90 to calcium in milk also doubled in 1963. At the same time, provided that further nuclear tests on the scale of those in the autumn of 1961 and 1962 do not take place, the danger to health as a result of such tests is considered negligible. We have by no means reached the danger level in these tests, and as long as the partial nuclear test ban treaty remains in force, it would appear that no ill-effects need be anticipated from the recent build-up of radiation.

It is reasonable to suppose that through radionics and radiesthesia we should be able to check the degree of radiation to which the population is exposed. Indeed in some cases radionic practitioners have already treated their patients for the elimination of radiation to which they have been exposed and rates have been worked out for the measurement of fall-out. How should we go about making tests for fall-out?

Supposing that we want to test a sample of milk for fall-out radiation, I suggest that we might go about the task in the following way. We place the sample of milk at 0cm. on the rule with our vial connection and radionic instrument at the 100cm. end. In an actual case, let us first put up the rate for calcium. It gave a reading of 48cm. Calcarea carb. 6 was then placed alongside the milk specimen, which gave a reading of 30cm., while Calcarea carb. 30 gave a reading of 25cm. This test was repeated with radioactive elements. The results of my test are tabulated below.

Calcium

	cm.
Calcium	48
With Calcarea carb. 6	30
With Calcarea carb. 30	25

Strontium

Strontium	48
With Strontium 30	21

Iodine

Iodine	48
With Iodum 6	40
With Iodum 30	30

Yttrium

Yttrium	46

Aluminium

Aluminium	46
With Alumina 6	37
With Alumina 30	37

I have included aluminium among the elements tested because it may help us to interpret the other readings, remembering always that in these tests we are measuring activation and not quantity as such. A person subject to aluminium poisoning would give a reading of over 50cm., signifying activation of aluminium in the system. If the milk had been warmed up in an aluminium pan, a similar reading might be expected, although this would depend to some extent on the quality of the pan. As it is, a reading of 46cm. can be taken as showing that the milk is not contaminated by aluminium. Alumina 6 lowers the reading to 37cm., which is not surprising when we remember that aluminium exists in natural form in plants and vegetables. But Alumina 30 does not lower the reading any further.

If we had been testing a human being instead of a milk sample and the rate for aluminium had given a reading of, say, 55cm., Alumina 30 would probably have provided a much lower reading and would have been useful for clearing the system of aluminium.

If we assume that the readings for calcium in this Grade A milk are near normal, it is interesting to see that while calcium is active as a constituent in the milk, with Calcarea carb. 6 lowering the reading by 18cm., it is not excessively so, as witness the fact that Calcarea carb. 30 only takes it down a further 5cm. When we come to strontium, however, we find that Strontium 30 takes the reading down to 21cm., from which we might deduce that strontium is more active than calcium. I had no Strontium 6 with which to test. The readings for iodine can be explained in the same way, the tests showing that iodine is active (perhaps we should say radioactive) in the milk. With radioactive strontium and iodine present in greater quantity in the milk (thus adding to its radioactivity), we might expect considerably lower readings when testing with Strontium 30 and Iodum 30. I have included yttrium as it is a subsidiary product of strontium and because some radionic practitioners apparently take steps to eliminate it rather than strontium when treating their patients for radiation. In this case its reading of 46cm. tells us that it is not a factor in any radioactive properties which the milk may have.

We can test a patient in much the same way as we can test an aliment like milk. We can put up the rate for strontium, obtain a reading, and then add the rate for bone. In an actual case the reading in both instances was 49cm. Strontium 30 reduced the reading on the rate for strontium from 49cm. to 24cm., while it reduced that for strontium in the bone to 18cm. It would appear that this lower reading is a measure of the activation, or radioactivity, of strontium in the bone. Naturally in a bad case of strontium toxaemia we should expect the reading for strontium in the bone to be higher than for strontium by itself. By using homoeopathic potencies we are able to detect the presence of strontium radioactivity in a rarefied form.

In a similar manner iodine gave a reading of 48cm. and the same reading for iodine in thyroid and bone respectively. Iodum 30 reduced the reading of 48cm. for iodine to 28cm., and for iodine in the bone to 30cm. But for iodine in the thyroid, Iodum 30 brought the reading right down to 15cm. These readings do suggest that this method of testing is valid and gives objective results. Its more precise value would have to be assessed over a considerable period of time.

If we wanted to treat a patient for radiation effects, we would of course proceed to find a remedy in the same way as we would in treating a virus or microbial infection. It has been suggested that the Schüssler salts could be useful in this connection, and as they are very efficient for toning up human tissue and eliminating toxins, it would seem to be good practice to test for the salts. Not only have we rates for all the elements but, in addition to strontium and iodine, potencies of radioactive elements such as caesium, cobalt and radium are available. There is also a remedy consisting of potentised X-rays, consisting of potentised alcohol previously exposed to X-rays. This could be useful in treating a patient for X-ray burns or one who has been over-exposed to these rays.

Rates for ultra-violet rays and electrical stimulation have been worked out, which might be useful for testing cases subject to an overdose of ultra-violet rays or who were suffering from electrical shock. In the treatment of radiation cases, the broadcasting method can be employed. Supposing it was decided to eliminate strontium, either the complementary rate of strontium or of strontium toxins (i.e. the rate for strontium preceded by the number 901) could be put on the instrument.

I have only been able to touch on this subject of radiation as one has had very little experience of it. But it is of particular interest to homoeopaths because, when we potentise a substance, we are in a sense making it radioactive. In eliminating an unwanted radiation, we are in effect matching the potency of the remedy to the strength of the radiation in just the same way as we match a remedy to the virulence of a virus or microbe.

This question of treating persons exposed to nuclear fall-out or excessive radiation is an all-important one and it is suggested that homoeopathy, radionics and radiesthesia have at least something, and perhaps much, to offer in this connection. I suspect that although it is the opinion of the experts that we are as yet nowhere near the danger threshold of nuclear fall-out, there are quite a few radionic practitioners who consider that even the slight radioactive doses to which we have all been exposed could be a factor in the health of a few highly sensitive people.

There is much to be done in this field and it is for the homoeopaths and radiesthetists to promote research along the road to which they are dedicated. If we ever have a nuclear war, which God forbid, perhaps some of us could best protect ourselves against the damaging effects of radiation by the provision of a potentised nuclear pill. Such an idea may not be nearly as far-fetched as it would sound to most people.

Chapter 12

Energy Levels in Elements and People

It will be appreciated from the previous chapter that potencies can be useful for identifying an element or compound in a particular substance. This can be further demonstrated by taking a sample of a vitamin preparation containing a number of minerals, calcium, phosphorus, iodine, also desiccated liver and bonemeal. Bonemeal itself contains in natural form a number of minerals such as copper, zinc, manganese and potassium.

I put a sample of the vitamin preparation at 0cm. on the rule and the rate for calcium on the instrument, attached to the 100cm. mark via the vial connection. I obtained a reading of 49cm. I then placed Calcarea carb. 6 in radiative contact with the vitamin preparation which gave a reading of 40cm., while Calcarea carb. 30 produced a reading of 37cm. I repeated this procedure for several other elements, the readings being as follows:

Calcium

	cm.
Calcium	49
With Calcarea carb. 6	40
With Calcarea carb. 30	37

Copper

Copper	49
With Cuprum 6	38
With Cuprum 30	30

Phosphorus

Phosphorus	49
With Phosphorus 6	35
With Phosphorus 30	29

Iodine

Iodine	49
With Iodum 6	38
With Iodum 30	28

Cobalt

| Cobalt | 47 |
| With Cobalt 30 | 44 |

Lead

Lead	48
With Plumbum 6	45
With Plumbum 30	44

It will be seen that while the potencies of calcium, copper, phosphorus and iodine lower the readings for these minerals by significant amounts, those for cobalt and lead have only a very slight effect on these minerals as represented by their rates. Through radiesthesia we know that everything occurring in nature radiates, and the lowering of the readings of a mineral brought about by potencies of that same mineral is an indication of its radiating power—an indication, in fact, of the presence of that mineral in the sample. Of the first four minerals tested, the drop in the readings for calcium when tested with potencies are less than those for copper, phosphorus and iodine. This may be explained by the fact that Calcarea carbonate is not a pure potency of calcium, but one of a calcium compound. It does not therefore activate the calcium in the sample to the same extent as a single potentised mineral would. Put in another way, we could say that it does not interfere with the normal radiation of calcium to the same extent.

The cobalt and lead potencies scarcely affect the readings for these minerals tested by themselves, the reason being that they are not present in the sample and cannot therefore be activated by potencies. It would seem from this experiment that we have here a simple and easy way of determining whether a particular element or compound is present in a substance, even in very small amounts, provided that we have samples of it in potentised form. Some indication is also given by the readings for the elements tested by themselves, the first four in the above case producing a reading of 49cm., while the cobalt and lead give slightly lower readings.

When working on the triangle we have a very simple method of assessing the freshness and quality of an aliment. Supposing that we want to test a sample of meat. We can place it at A on the triangle and take a measurement with the pendulum. If the meat is fresh and in good condition, the pendulum will oscillate along CD. As it begins to go stale, the reading will increase from 0° to 10°, then to 20° and so on, until it reaches a point of equilibrium.

I want now to go over very shortly a few points we should always remember when making a radiesthetic diagnosis. If we obtain a

P polarity reading above 38cm. (or whatever the individual practitioner takes as his normal balance point), the patient's system is definitely out of balance, which is invariably explained by the presence of some active infection. We might find at the same time urea giving a positive reaction (above 45cm. according to my own tests). If septicaemia gives a reading of over 50cm., the patient is very definitely toxic, and in all cases of parasitical infection in which the condition is of any importance, the reading for septicaemia will be positive to a greater or lesser amount. In a bad case it may go right up the scale.

I have made many references to tests on the P polarity. We can use it for diagnosis with the use of nosodes and for finding the suitability of drugs. Through it we can find what remedies are constitutionally suitable to a patient at the time of test, i.e. what remedies will add most to his vitality. By inference they should also correct any imbalance in his magnetic, or radiesthetic, field. They should help to restore the whole system to a state of what I would call magnetic balance, with every cell regarded as a battery in a state of electrical equilibrium. No drug well indicated on the P polarity should ever upset a patient. On the contrary it should always do some good. But having said that, it is important to notice that its indications have not quite the same precision that some other more detailed methods have, either on rule or triangle.

Supposing that we have a patient suffering from a severe cold. If we want to find quickly one or more appropriate remedies without going into detailed testing, we can test likely remedies on the P polarity. We may find that drugs like Aconite, Cinnamon and Baptisia are well indicated and go well together. Nevertheless, although improvement is very likely, the cold may persist, accompanied by debility. We may then test for infection on rule or triangle and get a strong reaction for measles, which may be measles toxins, for which the best remedy (tested, say, on the triangle) may be Gelsemium. This despite the fact that Gelsemium did not come out quite so well on the P polarity as the three remedies mentioned, perhaps providing a reading of 10cm. against 6cm. for the other three. The point I wish to reiterate is that while general tests such as those on the P polarity simply to find a remedy are extremely useful, especially where limited testing is either desired or only possible, in a professional sense nothing can take the place of detailed testing for infections and finding specific remedies to deal with them.

When we test nosodes on the P polarity, we are really testing them as remedies. If a patient has an acute attack of Asian influenza, we might expect that the homoeopathic nosode of that disease, i.e. the homoeopathic vaccine, would suit him well. In general terms this is so. For quick checks these nosodes are very useful and they can give a very good idea of what the patient is suffering from. Nevertheless there are one or two reservations which we should bear in mind. Take the case of a patient who has been having a course of homoeopathic treatment, say of 6c remedies, and it is desired to find out whether he still has any virus or bacterial toxins in his system. Testing the various nosodes on the P polarity may give readings of about 15cm. in every case, but if we test for an infection by putting up the rate for it on a radionic instrument and using the vial connection, we may obtain a positive reading. This is because, due to the treatment previously given, the energy level of the patient has been raised, and it would probably be found that for the time being all 30c remedies would also be contra-indicated. His system could have been overstimulated. If we tested him with 6c nosodes (provided we had them), or a 6c remedy which dealt effectively with an infection still active in his system, we could expect to get a favourable reading on the P polarity for the remedy and a positive one for one or other nosode, at say between 5 and 10cm. If we want to isolate any offending toxins and only have nosodes with which to do this, we can always test the nosodes on urea or on an affected organ. We could then expect to obtain readings below 10cm. for specific infections present in the system. At the same time the nosodes would not be suitable as remedies unless they measured up well on the P polarity.

One direction in which the P polarity is extremely useful is in deciding if a patient has had enough of any repetitive treatment. When the reading produced by a suitable drug rises to about 15cm., it is safe to say that it is no longer indicated and the patient has had enough of it. In all work of this kind we must not forget that we are sometimes dealing with a complicated case involving mixed infections where a certain amount of screening takes place. As treatment proceeds and more recent, and probably more superficial disease conditions, are removed from the system, new and older infections will show up positive on test. Remedies not previously indicated will be wanted to remove earlier and more deeply imbedded infections or toxins, which have been stirred up or activated as a result of the previous treatment. This process of removing the upper layers of disease is often illustrated in long-standing chronic cases. I can think of a skin case of twenty years standing which, after about a month's treatment, revealed active toxins of chicken-pox. The patient then told me that she had had what was considered a particularly bad attack of the disease at about the time when the skin trouble began. It is important to remove such poisons in the system, even if they are not the original cause of the symptoms from which the patient is suffering. One must work backwards in the endeavour finally to hit the jack-pot, the contamination (of whatever kind) which started the trouble.

During treatment one supervening disease condition or state is removed after another, and in that time the whole system is changed with resulting modification of the many radiations which contribute to the totality of the patient as a radiative being. Individual radiations or waveforms representing various imbalances, such as infections and affected organs, will go through a stage of transmogrification during this time. During treatment these subtle processes of change can be controlled through radiesthesia so that the patient's vitality is maintained with every prospect of a satisfactory outcome.

Chapter 13

Diseases and Their Remedies

Let us place a sample of pure aluminium strip in a small glass vial at 0cm. on the rule. If the rule is lying approximately East–West, we can obtain readings giving an indication of the energy content of substances and of potentised remedies. With myself facing south I found a balance point on the rule at 29cm. That was an R reading, which by definition is a reading obtained with only the object on test placed at 0cm. In the ordinary way we refer to R readings as being the first position on the rule, as we move the pendulum up the scale from 0cm., where it oscillates across the rule at right angles.

I repeated the test with potencies of aluminium or alumina, according to which I had available at the time. The results were as follows:

	cm.
Aluminium ϕ	29
Aluminium 3x	36
Alumina 6	38
Alumina 12	47
Alumina 30	58
Alumina 200	67
Aluminium CM	78

The same readings should be obtained with any other remedy or substance in potency, as they depend on their energy content and not on their identity. It will be observed that the sixth potency gives the same reading as the R reading for a human-being in normal health, i.e. 38cm. We can therefore assume that the 6c potency of a substance represents in some way the energy level, or vitality, of a human being.

One often refers to 3x potencies as being at the tissue level, as their dilution is only one in a thousand and their action is very much nearer that of allopathic drugs than higher potencies are. Their action is more akin to the chemical action of pure drugs and has a more or less direct effect on tissue substances. Here again the R reading is only slightly below that of a person in normal health.

Let us now orientate the rule North–South. With the 0cm. end of the rule pointing to the north with myself facing east, all potencies of aluminium gave the same reading of 41cm. In whatever potency Plumbum gave 53cm., Silica 55cm. and Cobalt 58cm., these readings thus giving an indication of *identity* and not energy. Facing west with the 0cm. end of the rule pointing to the south, aluminium potencies all gave a reading of 46cm. and Silica potencies one of 53cm. So that with the rule lying North–South, the readings are different according to which direction we are facing.

We now return the rule to the East–West position with the operator facing south, which is the way in which I ordinarily work. According to the layout of the room some operators may arrange their rules differently. If we put a sample of Alumina 30 at 0cm., we will again obtain a reading of 58cm. Let us now place in turn, in radiative contact with the Alumina 30, different potencies of Aluminium or Alumina according to which potencies we have available. Readings such as the following were obtained:

Alumina 30 at 0cm. with the following potencies in
radiative contact with it

	cm.
Aluminium 3x	19
Alumina 6	14
Alumina 12	12
Alumina 30	6
Aluminium 30	6
Alumina 200	15
Aluminium CM	25

It will be observed that Aluminium or Alumina 30 practically cuts out the *R* reading of Alumina 30 as might be expected, bringing the reading down to 6cm., and it is the only potency that does this.

If we are treating a patient and a remedy suits him well, it will give a low reading when tested on the *P* polarity. A 6c potency may reduce the reading to well under 10cm., while no other potency will do so. At the same time somewhat similar indications will be found without using *P* at all, i.e. with the patient's specimen on the rule and only the remedy alongside on a rubber block. The potency which is most suitable will give the lowest reading. But we must not forget that a slightly higher reading than the patient's normal *R* reading may also be found, as a good remedy will increase his vitality. Balance points can almost always be found at more than one position on the rule.

To return to the position where we have a 30c potency of Alumina on the rule at 0cm. We know that its *R* reading can be almost completely cut out on test by putting in radiative contact with it another sample of Alumina 30. If, instead of the Alumina 30 on the rule, we have the specimen of a patient who is suffering from aluminium poisoning, whose activation is of the order of a 30c potency, we will find that Alumina 30 placed in radiative contact with the specimen will provide a balance point somewhere below 10cm.

It is generally considered preferable in treating a case of aluminium poisoning not to administer Aluminium or Alumina in potency. If we could always get the dose exactly right, there would be nothing to be said against using it, but as aluminium is such an insidious metal and affects some people so badly, it is often thought preferable to use an antidote to the metal instead.

Let us again place our sample of Alumina 30 at 0cm. and then place Lycopodium 30 in radiative contact with it. The reading will come down to 6cm., thus cutting out the R reading of Alumina 30 as effectively as another sample of Alumina would do. It would thus seem that Lycopodium is the perfect antidote to aluminium poisoning. The actual potency of the remedy required in a case will depend upon the activation of the metal in the patient's system.

Since giving up aluminium in potency myself in order to clear a case of aluminium poisoning, I have always used Lycopodium and found it very effective. It has sometimes been suggested to me that another good antidote is Cadmium sulph. But on test Cadmium sulph. 30 will only reduce the R reading of Alumina 30 to 23. Plumbum has been used as an antidote, but Plumbum 30 on test produces a reading of 18. So it is more effective than Cadmium sulph., but less so than Lycopodium. In my opinion no remedy which does not reduce the R reading to 10cm. or under can be considered a satisfactory antidote.

It will be realised from the above considerations that we have here a method of finding out what remedies deal satisfactorily with various diseases and organisms as represented by their nosodes. The following results were obtained by using 30c nosodes and 30c remedies to antidote them. The lower the reading, the more effectively should the remedy deal with the organism in question. In one or two cases in which I had only 6c remedies, I used them instead of 30c remedies, making the necessary adjustments. Thus a 6c remedy, which provided a reading of 15cm., would give one of 9cm. when tested with a 30c remedy.

TABLE I

Syphilinum—Calc. fluorica 7, Calc. sulph 6, Hepar sulph 6, Kali phos 8, Kali sulph 5, Kalmia 9, Lycopodium 7, Mercurius cor 8, Mercurius sol 8, Penicillin 8.

Gonococcus—Calc. fluorica 7, Calc. sulph 8, Ferrum phos 6, Kali carb 10, Kali mur 10, Kali sulph 9, Lycopodium 5, Mercurius cor 9, Mercurius sol 9, Nat. sulph 9, Penicillin 5, Pulsatilla 7, Rhus tox 8, Sulphur 6, Thuja 7.

Medorrhinum—Calc. sulph 6, Hepar sulph 7, Kali phos 7, Kali sulph 9, Nat. sulph 7, Penicillin 8, Pulsatilla 10, Silica 7.

Tuberculins

Bacillinum—Calc. sulph 10, Rhus tox 5, Silica 7.

Tuberculinum—Arsenic iod 8, Crotalus 8, Lycopodium 8, Lycopus v. 8, Pulsatilla 6, Rhus tox 9, Sepia 8.

T.B. Bovinum—Arsenic iod 8, Crotalus 7, Drosera 8, Lachesis 10, Lycopodium 5, Nat. sulph 10, Pulsatilla 8.

T.B. Koch—Arsenic iod 7, Calc. phos 8, Crotalus 8, Kali phos 8, Pulsatilla 6, Silica 6.

Denys—Arsenic iod 5, Calc. sulph 8, Crotalus 9, Nat. sulph 6, Pulsatilla 5, Rhus tox 6, Sulphur 5.

Marmorek—Arsenic iod 8, Calc. sulph 10, Crotalus 9, Echinacea 6, Kali sulph 7, Lycopodium 7, Lycopus v. 9, Nat. sulph 8, Pulsatilla 6, Rhus tox 7, Sulphur 8.

Koch residue—Crotalus 9, Pulsatilla 6, Rhus tox 9.

Carcinosin—Acetic acid 7, Calc. iod 5, Card mar 9, Cobalt 10, Conium 7, Crotalus 8, Eucalyptus 9, Euphorbium 10, Fuligo 9, Lapis albus 6, Lobelia erinus 10, Lobelia inflata 6, Lycopodium 9, Rhus tox 10, Sulphur 7, Symphytum 5, Taraxacum 9, Uranium nit 7.

Rous sarcoma—Acetic acid 10, Apocynam 7, Calc. iod 7, Card. mar 7, Conium 8, Crotalus 7, Euphorbium 7, Fuligo 7, Lapis albus 6, Lobelia inflata 6, Lycopodium 10, Ornithogalum 7, Ruta 8, Sepia 7, Sulphur 7, Symphytum 7, Uranium nit 7.

Scirrhinum—Acetic acid 9, Calc. sulph 10, Fuligo 9, Kali sulph 9, Lachesis 9, Lapis albus 9, Magnesium phos 8, Sulphur 8.

Streptococci

Strep. co.—Calc. sulph 6, Crotalus 6, Ferrum phos 7, Kali mur 9, Kali sulph 8, Lachesis 7, Lycopodium 9, Nat. phos 8, Sulphur 7, Tarentula cub 5, Vipera 7.

S. haemolyticus—Calc. sulph 9, Crotalus 9, Kali sulph 8, Lachesis 9, Lycopodium 9, Penicillin 9, Rhus tox 5, Sulphur 8, Tarentula cub 10.

S. pyogenes—Calc. sulph 5, Kali sulph 5, Lachesis 5, Lycopodium 6, Penicillin 5, Rhus tox 7, Sulphur 7, Tarentula cub 5.

S. rheumaticus—Calc. sulph 5, Crotalus 6, Sulphur 7, Tarentula cub 5.

S. viridans—Calc. sulph 9, Crotalus 6, Kali sulph 6, Lachesis 5, Penicillin 6, Rhus tox 5, Sepia 8, Sulphur 5, Tarentula cub 5.

Staphylococci

Staph. co.—Calc. sulph 6, Hepar sulph 6, Stannum met 6, Tarentula cub 5.

S. abdominalis—Hepar sulph 8, Kali mur 7, Magnesium phos 8, Nat. mur 8, Nat. sulph 7, Tarentula cub 8.

S. aureus—Calc. sulph 6, Hepar sulph 7, Kali sulph 9, Stannum met 5, Sulphur 10, Tarentula cub 5.

S. haem. aureus—Calc. sulph 5, Graphites 8, Kali sulph 7, Sepia 9, Stannum met 7, Tarentula cub 5.

S. pyogenes—Calc. sulph 9, Hepar sulph 5, Nat. sulph 8, Rhus tox 8, Stannum met 8, Sulphur 6, Tarentula cub 5.

Enterococcus—Hepar sulph 6, Vipera 8.

Pneumococcus—Aconite n. 6, Bryonia 6, Causticum 6, Phosphorus 6.

Bowel organisms

B. coli—Berberis 5, Cantharides 5, Causticum 5, Colchicum 6, Granatum 5, Ignatia 8, Ipecac. 6, Podophyllum 5, Silica 5.

B. typhosus coli—Anacardium 7, Arsenic alb 7, Baptisia 6, Kali mur 6.

B. faecalis alkaligenes (Bach)—Kali sulph 7, Lycopodium 8, Sepia 5, Sulphur 9.

B. Gaertner—Elaps cor 7, Sepia 7, Sulphur 10.

B. Morgan—Calc. sulph 10, Card. mar 5, Crotalus 6, Kali phos 7, Lachesis 8, Rhus tox 9, Sulphur 8.

Morgan-Gaertner (Paterson)—Ant. crud 8, Rhus tox 7, Vipera 8.

B. Mutabile (Bach)—Ant. crud 7, Calc. phos 10, Kali phos 8, Lachesis 10, Nat. sulph 9, Sepia 10.

B. Proteus—Argent nit 8, Calc. phos 8, Card. mar 9, Hepar sulph 7, Nat. mur 7.

Sycotic—Lachesis 9, Magnesium phos 10, Mercury cor 10, Mercury sol 10, Nat. mur 10, Penicillin 7, Pulsatilla 9, Rhus tox 10, Sepia 7, Thuja 8.

Bacillinum No. 7 (Paterson)—Calc. iod 6, Causticum 10, Crotalus 7, Kali bich 7, Kali mur 6, Lachesis 7, Lycopodium 7, Sulphur 10.

Bacillinum No. 10 (Paterson)—Arsenic alb 8, Sulphur 7, Vipera 7.

Typhi—Anacardium 6, Arsenic alb 8, Baptisia 5, Kali mur 5.

Paratyphi—Anacardium 7, Arsenic alb 8, Baptisia 7, Kali mur 8.

T.A.B.C.—Arsenic alb 7, Baptisia 6, Bryonia 7, Kali phos 8, Phosphorus 10, Vipera 7.

Dysentery co.—Arsenic alb 6, Ipecac. 7, Kali sulph 8, Mercury cor 9, Vipera 8.

Dysentery (Bach)—Arsenic alb 5, Hepar sulph 10, Ipecac. 8, Mercury sol 10, Sulphur 9.

B. Welchii—Aluminium 10, Carbo veg 7, Phosphorus 8, Rhus tox 10.

B. Botulinum—Aluminium 6, Carbo veg 9, Nat. mur 8, Rhus tox 6.

B. tetani—Argent nit 8, Pulsatilla 10, Sepia 9, Silica 7.

Diptherinum—Aconite n. 9, Belladonna 8, Calc. fluorica 7, Calc. sulph 10, Echinacea 8, Ferrum phos 5, Gelsemium 7, Kali sulph 9, Nat. sulph 7, Sulphur 5.

Calf diptheria—Crotalus 10, Echinacea 7, Hepar sulph 7, Kali mur 8, Kali phos 6, Kali sulph 7, Lachesis 8, Magnesium phos 10, Nat. sulph 10.

Vaccinium—Kali phos 8, Silica 8, Thuja 10.

Anthracinum—Calc. sulph 7, Crotalus 7, Echinacea 9, Kali carb 10, Nat. phos 10, Nat. sulph 5, Tarentula cub 7, Vipera 10.

Hydrophobia—Aconite n. 7, Arsenic alb 10, Crotalus 8, Ferrum phos 5, Kali phos 10, Latyrus 8, Pulsatilla 8, Stramonium 10, Vipera 7.

Malaria—Arsenic alb 6, Chininium sulph 7, Cinchona 8, Lachesis 5, Malaria officinalis 7.

B. pestis—Lycopodium 8, Sepia 9.

Psorinum—Kali mur 6, Silica 9, Sulphur 8.

Pyrogen—Calc. sulph 5, Crotalus 7, Echinacea 5, Kali phos 7, Kali sulph 10, Magnesium phos 5, Nat. sulph 7, Penicillin 9, Sulphur 8.

Septicaemin—Calc. fluor 8, Echinacea 6, Kali phos 8, Kali sulph 6, Nat. sulph 6, Sulphur 5.

Variolinum—Crotalus 7, Echinacea 8, Gelsemium 5.

Influenzas

Virus A—Aconite n. 8, Cinnamon 10, Gelsemium 8, Kali phos 8.

Virus B—Aconite n. 8, Calc. phos 10, Cinnamon 8, Gelsmium 6, Kali phos 7.

Asian—Aconite lycot 6, Aconite n. 9, Cinnamon 7, Gelsemium 7, Kali phos 8.

Spanish—Aconite lycot 9, Bryonia 9, Calc. phos 10, Kali phos 6.

Mucobacter—Aconite n. 6, Arsenic alb 6, Calc. phos 6, Causticum 4, Ferrum phos 10, Kali mur 6, Kali sulph 10, Nat. sulph 10, Phosphorus 6, Pulsatilla 10.

B. bronchisepticus—Aconite lycot 7, Calc. phos 9, Kali mur 7, Kali phos 6, Nat. mur 10.

B. influenzae—Aconite lycot 8, Aconite n. 8, Belladonna 8, Cinnamon 9, Ferrum phos 9, Gelsemium 10, Kali mur 5, Nat. mur 7, Nat. phos 10.

Cornybacterium coryzae—Aconite n. 8, Arsenic alb 5, Calc. phos 8, Cinnamon 10, Kali phos 7, Nat. mur 7, Sabadilla 7.

Haemolytic influenzae—Belladonna 7, Bryonia 7, Ferrum phos 8, Kali phos 10.

B. Koch-Weeks—Aconite lycot 10, Aconite n. 6, Allium cepa 10, Arsenic alb 9, Bryonia 10, Calc. carb 7, Causticum 6, Ferrum phos 6, Gelsemium 10, Kali phos 7, Nat. mur 9, Phosphorus 10, Pulsatilla 5.

B. Morax-Axenfeldt—Aconite n. 9, Ferrum phos 9, Gelsemium 7, Kali mur 7, Kali phos 9, Phosphorus 10, Pulsatilla 9, Rhus tox 7.

Aseptic meningitis—Calc. phos 7, Kali phos 9.

Encephalitis—Aconite lycot 5, Bryonia 10, Cinnamon 5, Kali phos 8.

Meningitis—Calc. sulph 10, Gelsemium 7, Kali phos 8, Lachesis 7, Silica 8, Sulphur 6.

Poliomyelitis—Aconite n. 8, Calc. phos 7, Cannabis indica 7, Gelsemium 10, Ignatia 7, Kali mur 7, Kali phos 7, Latyrus 6, Phosphorus 5, Sulphur 7, Vipera 5.

Psittacosis—Belladonna 9, Calc. phos 8, Gelsemium 10, Kali carb 10, Kali phos 9.

T.B. meningitis—Aconite lycot 8, Calc. sulph 5, Crotalus 7, Lachesis 9, Pulsatilla 7.

Epidemic diseases

Morbillinum (measles)—Aconite n. 7, Belladonna 6, Gelsemium 7, Pulsatilla 10.

Parotidinum (mumps)—Aconite n. 9, Ant. tart 9, Belladonna 8, Ferrum phos 8, Kali sulph 10, Magnesium phos 8, Pulsatilla 6.

Pertussis (whooping cough)—Aconite n. 6, Belladonna 7, Calc. phos 7, Calc. sulph 9, Gelsemium 5, Kali mur 10, Kali phos 8, Nat. phos 9, Nat. sulph 6, Silica 6.

Rubella (German measles)—Aconite n. 9, Belladonna 6, Kali sulph 8, Nat. mur 10, Nat. sulph 6, Rhus tox 7, Tarentula cub 7.

Scarlatina—Aconite lycot 10, Aconite n. 7, Belladonna 9, Kali mur 7, Nat. sulph 7, Rhus tox 6.

Varicella (chicken pox)—Aconite n. 7, Belladonna 5, Gelsemium 8, Rhus tox 8.

Skin diseases

B. acne—Arsenic alb 10, Arsenic iod 8, Calc. carb 6, Calc. fluor 8, Calc. phos 9, Calc. sulph 8, Ferrum phos 8, Nat. sulph 8, Rhus tox 6, Sulphur 10.

Erysipelas—Apis 10, Cantharides 8, Crotalus 5, Rhus tox 9, Stannum met 10, Veratrum vir 9.

Herpes simplex—Echinacea 10, Hepar sulph 10, Sepia 8, Sulphur 10, Tellurium 7.

Herpes zoster—Echinacea 5, Sulphur 5, Tellurium 8.

Tinea pedis (athlete's foot)—Calc. carb 9, Calc. phos 10, Calc. sulph 9, Causticum 9, Kali mur 9, Nat. mur 10, Nat. phos 8, Stannum met 10, Vipera 7.

B. Hodgkini—Ant. crud 10, Echinacea 10, Graphites 8, Kali mur 10, Kali phos 7, Lycopodium 10, Nat. mur 10, Nat. phos 7, Rhus tox 6, Sulphur 8.

TABLE II

Acetic acid—*Carcinosin,* Rous sarcoma, Scirrhinum.

Aconite lycotonum—B. influenzae, *Bronchisepticus, M. catarrhalis, Encephalitis, Hydrophobia,* Influenzae *Asian* & Spanish, Koch-Weeks, Scarlatina, T.B. meningitis.

Aconitum n.—B. influenzae, M. catarrhalis, Cornybacterium coryzae, Diphtherinum, Influenzae Asian, virus A and B, *Koch-Weeks,* Morax, *Morbillinum, Mucobacter,* Parotidinum, *Pertussis,* Poliomyelitis, *Pneumococcus,* Rubella, *Scarlatina, Varicella.*

Allium cepa—Koch-Weeks.

Aluminium—*Botulinum,* Welchii.

Anacardium—*Paratyphoid, Typhoid, B. typhosus coli.*

Antimony crud.—B. Hodgkini, *Mutabile.*

Antimony tart.—M. catarrhalis, Morgan-Gaertner (Paterson), Parotidinum.

Apis mel.—Erysipelas.

Apocynam—Carcinosin, *Rous sarcoma.*

Argent nit.—B. Proteus, Tetanus.

Arsenic alb.—B. acne, Bac. No. 10 (Paterson), *Cornybacterium coryzae, Dysentery (Bach), Dysentery co.,* Hydrophobia, Koch-Weeks, *Malaria, Mucobacter,* Paratyphoid, *T.A.B.C.,* Typhoid, *B. typhosus coli.*

Arsenic iod.—B. acne, *Diphtherinum,* T.B. bovinum, *Denys,* Koch & Marmorek, Tuberculinum.

Baptisia—*Paratyphoid, T.A.B.C., Typhoid, B. typhosus coli.*

Belladonna—B. influenzae, Diptherinum, *H. influenzae, Morbillinum,* Parotidinum, *Pertussis,* Psittacosis, *Rubella,* Scarlatina, *Varicella.*

Berberis—*B. coli.*

Bryonia—*M. catarrhalis*, Encephalitis, *H. influenzae*, Influenza Spanish, Koch-Weeks, *Pneumococcus, T.A.B.C.*

Calcarea carb.—*B. acne*, M. catarrhalis, *Koch-Weeks*, Tinea pedis.

Calcarea fluorica—B. acne, *Diphtherinum, Gonococcus,* Septicaemin, *Syphilinum.*

Calcarea iod.—*Bac. No. 7 (Paterson), Carcinosin, Rous sarcoma.*

Calcarea phos.—B. acne, *Aseptic meningitis,* Bronchisepticus, Cornybacterium coryzae, Influenzae virus B & Spanish, Meningitis, *Mucobacter,* Mutabile, *Pertussis, Poliomyelitis,* B. Proteus, Psittacosis, T.B. Koch, Tinea pedis.

Calcarea sulph.—B. acne, *Anthracinum,* Bacillinum, Diphtherinum, Gonococcus, *Medorrhinum,* Meningitis, B. Morgan, Pertussis, *Pyrogen,* Scirrhinum, *Staph. aureus, Staph. H. aureus, Staph. co.,* Staph. pyogenes, *Strep. co., Strep. haem., Strep. pyogenes, Strep. rheumaticus,* Strep. viridans, *Syphilinum,* T.B. Denys, *T.B. meningitis,* T.B. Marmorek, Tinea pedis.

Cannabis indica—*Poliomyelitis.*

Cantharides—*B. coli,* Erysipelas.

Carbo veg.—Botulinum, *B. Welchii.*

Carduus mar.—Carcinosin, *B. Morgan,* B. Proteus, *Rous sarcoma.*

Causticum—*M. catarrhalis,* Bacil. No. 7 (Paterson), *B. coli, Koch-Weeks, Mucobacter, Pneumococcus,* Tinea pedis.

Chininium sulph.—*Malaria.*

Cinchona—Malaria.

Cinnamon—B. influenzae, M. catarrhalis, Cornybacterium, coryzae, *Encephalitis,* Influenzae virus A, B & *Asian.*

Cobalt—Carcinosin.

Colchicum—*B. coli.*

Conium—*Carcinosin,* Rous sarcoma.

Crotalus—*Anthracinum, Bacil. No. 7 (Paterson),* Calf diphtheria, Carcinosin, *Erysipelas,* Hydrophobia, Koch residue, *B. Morgan, Pyrogen, Rous sarcoma, Strep. co.,* Strep. haem., *Strep. rheumaticus, Strep. viridans, T.B. bovinum,* T.B. Denys, Koch, Marmorek, *T.B. meningitis,* Tuberculinum, *Variolinum.*

Drosera—T.B. bovinum.

Echinacea—Anthracinum, *Calf diphtheria,* Diphtherinum, Herpes simplex, *Herpes zoster,* B. Hodgkini, *Marmorek, Pyrogen, Septicaemin,* Variolinum.

Elaps cor.—*B. Gaertner.*

Euphorbium—Carcinosin, *Rous sarcoma.*

Ferrum phos.—B. acne, B. influenzae, *Diphtherinum, Gonococcus, Hydrophobia,* H. influenzae, *Koch-Weeks,* Morax, Mucobacter, Parotidinum, *Strep. co.*

H

Fuligo—Carcinosin, *Rous sarcoma*, Scirrhinum.

Gelsemium—B. influenzae, *Diphtherinum*, Influenzae virus A, *B &
Asian*, Koch-Weeks, *Meningitis, Morax, Morbillinum, Pertussis*,
Poliomyelitis, Psittacosis, Varicella, *Variolinum*.

Granatum—*B. coli*.

Graphites—B. Hodgkini, Staph. H. aureus.

Hepar sulph.—*Calf diphtheria*, Dysentery (Bach), *Enterococcus*,
Herpes simplex, *Medorrhinum, B. Proteus*, Staph. abdominalis,
Staph. aureus, Staph. co., Staph. pyogenes, Syphilinum.

Ignatia—B. coli, *Poliomyelitis*.

Ipecac.—*B. coli*, Dysentery (Bach), *Dysentery co*.

Kali bich.—*Bacil. No. 7 (Paterson)*.

Kali carb.—Anthracinum, Gonococcus, Psittacosis.

Kali mur—*Bacil. No. 7 (Paterson), B. influenzae, Bronchisepticus*,
Calf diphtheria, Gonococcus, B. Hodgkini, *Morax, Mucobacter*,
Paratyphoid, Pertussis, *Poliomyelitis, Psorinum, Scarlatina, Staph.
abdominalis*, Strep. co., Tinea pedis, *Typhoid, B. typhosus coli*.

Kali phos.—Aseptic meningitis, *Bronchisepticus, Calf diphtheria, M.
catarrhalis, Cornybacterium coryzae, Diphtherinum*, Encephalitis,
B. Hodgkini, Hydrophobia, H. influenzae, Influenzae virus A, *B,
Asian & Spanish, Koch-Weeks, Medorrhinum*, Meningitis, Morax,
B. Morgan, Mutabile, Pertussis, *Poliomyelitis*, Psittacosis, *Pyrogen*,
Septicaemin, Syphilinum, T.A.B.C., T.B. Koch, Vaccinium.

Kali sulph.—*Calf diphtheria*, Diphtherinum, Dysentery co., *Faecalis*,
Gonococcus, *Marmorek*, Medorrhinum, Mucobacter, Parotidinum, Pyrogen, Rubella, Scirrhinum, *Septicaemin, Staph. H.
aureus*, Staph. pyogenes, Strep. co., Strep. haem., *Strep. pyogenes,
Strep. viridans, Syphilinum*.

Kalmia—Syphilinum.

Lachesis—*Bacil. No. 7* (Paterson), Calf diphtheria, *Malaria*, Marmorek, *Meningitis*, B. Morgan, B. Mutabile, Scirrhinum, *Strep.
co.*, Strep. haem., *Strep. pyogenes, Strep. viridans*, Sycotic, T.B.
bovinum, T.B. meningitis.

Lapis albus—*Carcinosin, Rous sarcoma*, Scirrhinum.

Latyrus—Hydrophobia, *Poliomyelitis*.

Lycopodium—*Bacil. No. 7 (Paterson)*, Carcinosin, Faecalis, *Gonococcus*, B. Hodgkini, *Marmorek*, B. pestis, Rous sarcoma, Strep.
co., Strep. haem., *Strep. pyogenes, Syphilinum, T.B. bovinum*,
Tuberculinum.

Lycopus v.—Marmorek, Tuberculinum.

Lobelia erinata—Carcinosin.

Lobelia inflata—*Carcinosin, Rous sarcoma*.

Magnesium phos.—Calf diphtheria, Parotidinum, *Pyrogen*, Scirrhinum, Staph. abdominalis, Sycotic.

Malaria offic.—*Malaria.*

Mercurius cor.—*Diphtherinum,* Dysentery co., Gonococcus, Sycotic, Syphilinum.

Mercurius cyanide—*Calf diphtheria, Diphtherinum.*

Mercurius sol—*Diphtherinum,* Dysentery (Bach), Gonococcus, Sycotic, Syphilinum.

Natrum mur—*B. influenzae,* Botulinum, Bronchisepticus, *M. catarrhalis, Cornybacterium coryzae,* B. Hodgkini, Koch-Weeks, *B. Proteus,* Rubella, Staph. abdominalis, Sycotic, Tinea pedis.

Natrum phos.—Anthracinum, *B. Hodgkini,* B. influenzae, Pertussis, Strep. co., Tinea pedis.

Natrum sulph.—B. acne, *Anthracinum,* Calf diphtheria, *Denys, Diphtherinum,* Gonococcus, Marmorek, *Medorrhinum, Mucobacter,* Mutabile, *Pertussis, Pyrogen, Rubella, Scarlatina, Septicaemin, Staph. abdominalis,* Staph. pyogenes, T.B. bovinum.

Ornithogalum—*Rous sarcoma.*

Penicillin calcium—*Gonococcus,* Medorrhinum, Pyrogen, *Strep. co.,* Strep. haem., *Strep. pyogenes, Strep. viridans, Sycotic,* Syphilinum.

Phosphorus—Koch-Weeks, *Morax, Mucobacter, Pneumococcus, Poliomyelitis,* B. Welchii, T.A.B.C.

Podophyllum—*B. coli.*

Pulsatilla—*Gonococcus,* Hydrophobia, *Koch-Weeks, Koch residue,* Medorrhinum, Morax, Morbillinum, Mucobacter, *Parotidinum,* Sycotic, T.B. bovinum, *Denys, Koch & Marmorek, T.B. meningitis,* Tetanus, *Tuberculinum.*

Rhus tox—*B. acne, Bacillinum, Bacil. No. 7 (Paterson), Botulinum,* Carcinosin, *Denys,* Erysipelas, Gonococcus, *B. Hodgkini,* Koch residue, Koch-Weeks, *Marmorek, Morax,* B. Morgan, *Morgan-Gaertner (Paterson),* Pyrogen, *Rubella, Scarlatina,* Staph. pyogenes, *Strep. haem., Strep. pyogenes, Strep. viridans,* Sycotic, Tuberculinum, Varicella, B. Welchii.

Ruta—Carcinosin, Rous sarcoma.

Sabadilla—*M. catarrhalis, Cornybacterium coryzae, Koch-Weeks.*

Sepia—*B. Gaertner, Faecalis,* Herpes simplex, Mutabile, B. pestis, *Rous sarcoma,* Staph. H. aureus, Strep. viridans, *Sycotic,* Tetanus, Tuberculinum.

Silica—*Bacillinum, B. coli, T.B. Koch, Medorrhinum,* Meningitis, *Pertussis,* Psorinum, *Tetanus,* Vaccinium.

Stannum met.—Erysipelas, *Staph. aureus, Staph. co., Staph. H. aureus,* Staph. pyogenes, Tinea pedis.

Stramonium—Hydrophobia.

Sulphur—B. acne, Bacil. No. 7 (Paterson), *Bacil. No. 10 (Paterson), Carcinosin, Diphtherinum,* Dysentery (Bach), B. Faecalis, B.

Gaertner, *Gonococcus*, Herpes simplex, *Herpes zoster*, B. Hodg-kini, *Meningitis*, B. Morgan, *Poliomyelitis*, Psorinum, Pyrogen, *Rous sarcoma*, Scirrhinum, *Septicaemin*, Staph. aureus, *Staph. pyogenes, Strep. co., Strep. haem., Strep. pyogenes, Strep. rheumaticus*, Strep. viridans, T.B. *Denys*, Koch & Marmorek.

Symphytum—*Carcinosin, Rous sarcoma.*

Tarentula cubensis—*Anthracinum, Rubella*, Staph. abdominalis, *Staph. aureus, Staph. co., Staph. H. aureus, Staph. pyogenes, Strep. co., Strep. haem., Strep. pyogenes, Strep. viridans.*

Tellurium—*Herpes simplex*, Herpes zoster.

Taraxacum—Carcinosin.

Thuja—Sycotic, Vaccinium.

Uranium nit.—*Carcinosin, Rous sarcoma.*

Veratrum vir.—Erysipelas.

Vipera—Anthracinum, *Bacil. No. 10 (Paterson)*, Diptherinum, Dysentery co., Enterococcus, *Hydrophobia*, Morgan-Gaertner (Paterson), *Poliomyelitis, Strep. co., T.A.B.C., Tinea pedis.*

Table I gives the various pathogenic organisms with the remedies which deal with them. Table II shows at a glance each remedy with the virus or microbial infections on which it acts. In Table I the best remedies as found on test for dealing with a pathogen are those giving a reading of 7 or under, while those giving a reading of 8 to 10 are less well indicated. In Table II remedies giving a reading of from 5 to 7 when tested against an organism are printed in italics. Naturally these results take no account of the constitution of a patient for whom a remedy has to be found. Generally speaking we can assume that the lower the reading, the more often will the remedy be required for dealing with the infection treated. But equally one of the less well indicated remedies may be needed, depending on the constitution of the patient, other organisms which may be in his system and its state of intoxication. It may even be that a remedy which could not be included in Table I may be needed at times. As must now be clear to the reader, it is often desirable to find a remedy to deal at one and the same time with more than one infection. It is hoped that the tables will help the practitioner in his choice of such a remedy.

Some practitioners are great believers in the Schüssler salts and, partly for this reason, the salts were tested for almost every organism dealt with. I must confess to being somewhat surprised at finding how very well these salts reacted for many of the organisms, and it may be that they should be used more often than they are by homoeopaths. It will be realised that owing to the large number of successive tests involved in getting out such tables, when a reading is checked a second time, it may not produce exactly the same number. It may come out the second time as 7 instead of 6; the discrepancy may be even greater. Nevertheless I am of the opinion that the numbers do serve a useful purpose and do give a fairly accurate idea of the *relative* importance of the different remedies listed for dealing with a specific organism.

In choosing remedies to test, the author largely restricted himself to the better-known remedies, or those which he had particular reason for believing would deal with the organism under consideration. Other practitioners can add to the list of remedies according to their own experience or tests as they think fit. When a remedy reduces the *R* reading of an organism substantially to any number under 10, we could say that there is a harmonic relationship between them. We come back to the idea of syntonisation between drug and organism.

Medical practitioners may be interested in the results obtained by testing four antibiotic drugs in the same manner. This was made possible by the fact that these drugs are obtainable in potentised form. The results are given in Table III.

TABLE III

Tetracycline—*Anthrax*, B. Hodgkini, Pneumococcus, *Strep. haem.*, *Strep. pyogenes*, *Strep. rheumaticus*, T.A.B.C.

Chlortetracycline—B. Hodgkini, *Strep. co.*, T.A.B.C., Tinea pedis.

Streptomycin—*Herpes simplex*, B. Hodgkini, Marmorek, Morgan-Gaertner (Paterson), *Pneumococcus*, *Staph. H. aureus*, Strep. haem., Strep. viridans, T.A.B.C.

Oxytetracycline—*Enterococcus*, Herpes simplex, Marmorek, Pneumococcus, Strep. co., *Strep. pyogenes*, Strep. viridans, *Syphilinum*, T.A.B.C.

•

It is well known that the action of a potentised homoeopathic remedy is not the same as that of the remedy in unpotentised, or pure, form. Nevertheless, it is hoped that these tests do give some indication of the organisms with which the drugs deal effectively, whether potentised or not. In Table III the organisms which produced readings of 7 or under when tested against the respective drugs are shown in italics.

It is interesting to notice how the results in these tables confirm established practice in many respects and at the same time suggest a new emphasis for the use of certain drugs when dealing with specific organisms. It may surprise some to see how well Pulsatilla shows up in dealing with the various tuberculins. The best remedies on test for dealing with the cancer nosode diseases are Calc. iod., Lapis albus, Lobelia inflata and Symphytum. An advantage of Calcarea sulph. is that it can deal effectively with both streptococcal and staphylococcal infections. Its value was brought home to the author personally in a positive way when it finally cleared up a very nasty septic foot he had, which persisted despite a course of penicillin treatment.

It would appear from the table that more emphasis might be laid on Tarentula cubensis for such affections. In testing Tarentula the author had in mind the fact that the late Dr. Dorothy Shepherd always prescribed Tarentula for boils, with persistently good results. Rhus tox. and Sulphur are of course primary remedies for streptococcal infections, while Hepar sulph. and Stannum show up very well for staphylococci, as might be expected.

One could go on commenting at length. When one remembers that Pyrogen represents pus, the four remedies indicated so strongly for this condition may be useful. Cinnamon, which Dr. Guyon Richards used so extensively for influenza, is indicated for Influenza virus A, B and Asian, but when tested against Spanish influenza, the reading was 15! On the other hand Kali phos. deals effectively with all the influenzas, according to the table.

One might have expected the two nosodes labelled 'B. Influenzae' and 'Haemolytic Influenzae' to require very much the same remedies, but they do differ quite considerably. In practice it may be useful to employ both for testing. When we come to the epidemic diseases, it is not surprising that Aconitum and Belladonna figure so prominently. They certainly helped to convince me of the validity of these tests. It remains to be said that if the tables can assist the practitioner in his choice of remedies for dealing with specific organisms, the final assessment must depend on the tests he is able to make on the specimens of his patients.

Chapter 14

Organs and Their Remedies

Having found remedies which should deal effectively with various pathogenic organisms, I decided to try to find a similar method of discovering remedies which have an affinity with the various bodily organs, i.e. remedies whose vibrations were in tune with the organs so that they would provide a very definite stimulation to them and tone them up. For this purpose I employed Turenne witnesses.

Following a number of tests, I came to the conclusion that I could do this by testing the witnesses on their P polarity with 6c remedies. I placed the witness at 0cm. with P on a rubber block on one side of the witness and each remedy in turn on the other side, in exactly the same way as if I was testing a patient for suitable remedies. I made a list of all those remedies which provided readings of 12cm. or under.

In testing a patient in this way we know that we are finding a remedy which provides a wanted stimulus for the patient, which is constitutional to him at the time of test and which is dealing with an infection, or some other imbalance, in his system. We can say that he is deficient in the remedy's vibration and that in restoring it to his system, we are tending to bring his system up to a normal state of balance. There is in fact resonance between the remedy and the patient's witness. Otherwise the remedy would have no effect.

In a similar manner, in testing organs on the P polarity, we are again finding which remedies provide some kind of relationship or resonance with the organ, but in this case the action is simply one of providing energy to the organ, i.e. of stimulating it or toning it up. We can demonstrate the principle by putting a sample of pure aluminium at 0cm. and testing it out on its P polarity, i.e. with P on one side of it on a rubber block and the potencies to be tested on the other side. The P polarity reading was 22cm.

There is no more efficient way of stimulating an organ, or activating a substance, than by employing a potency of itself. This principle applies in the case of nosodes, which are potencies of the disease organisms which they are designed to destroy. By supplying the necessary degree of resonance, they stimulate the organism to the point of disintegration.

Aluminium ϕ on P polarity
(Rule balance point = 22)

	cm.
Aluminium 6	10
Alumina 6	12
Lycopodium 6	10
Cadmium sulph 6	20
Cuprum 6	17
Stannum met. 6	17
Plumbum 6	17
Sulphur 6	15

In the above table it will be seen that Aluminium 6 reduces the reading to 10. It is not surprising that Alumina 6, the oxide of aluminium, reduces the reading only to 12 because, although it is very similar to aluminium, it is not of course the same. What is perhaps surprising is that Lycopodium 6 also gives a reading of 10. This confirms Lycopodium as probably the most suitable remedy there is for eliminating aluminium from the system of a patient. It is what I have always used myself since giving up aluminium or alumina in potency for this purpose. On the other hand Cadmium sulph., which is sometimes recommended for the elimination of aluminium, produced a reading of 20. As this is exactly twice the reading of that for aluminium, there may conceivably be some sort of harmonic relationship between Cadmium sulph. and Aluminium of some significance. I do not think myself that Cadmium sulph. could ever take the place of Lycopodium. One or two other readings are given for purposes of comparison.

I orientated the sample of Aluminium ϕ on the rule so that in any re-testing, conditions were as far as possible the same. At the same time orientation did not appear to make any measurable difference to the readings. In getting out the results embodied in the following tables, I placed each Turenne witness in turn in a glass vial approximately 2cm. in diameter and 9cm. long. The idea of using a glass vial was to intensify the signal given out by the witness, using it in fact as a resonance chamber. In checking some of the results I came to the conclusion that this vial was not very satisfactory and I repeated all the tests with a vial approximately 2½cm. in diameter and 5½cm. long. The result was to lower the readings somewhat and, in fact, most of the final readings came within the range of 6 to 10. I orientated the vial containing the witness in each case so that, in checking the results, the conditions were as far as possible the same. The top of the vial was left open.

In checking and re-checking the readings, it was obvious that one could not expect to obtain exactly the same readings in every case. The slightest extraneous influence could affect the results. Nevertheless I came to the conclusion that the general principles and method of testing was sound and that the readings did indicate suitable remedies for syntonising with the organs tested.

I arranged the remedies in an order of priorities so that those which gave the lowest readings come first, while those which were least well indicated come last. Remedies which gave the same readings are placed in alphabetical order. The actual range of readings is shown under each organ, so that it can be easily determined what actual or approximate reading any particular remedy gave. It should be understood, however, that too much importance should not be placed on the order in which the drugs are given. The intention was to find likely remedies which could be used for stimulating an organ lacking in function.

TABLE I

Organs and their remedies

Blood (normal) (8–11)—Ferrum phos., Arsenic alb., Kali mur, Kali phos., Nat. mur., Nat. phos., Nat. sulph, Sepia, Rhus tox.

Heart (10–12)—Digitalis, Cactus, Kalmia, Aconite, Anacardium, Arnica, Arsenic alb., Gelsemium, Lycopodium, Spigelia.

Aorta (8–12)—Arnica, Spigelia, Arsenic alb., Cactus, Anacardium, Digitalis, Gelsemium, Iris v., Kalmia, Calc. phos., Lycopodium.

Medulla obl. (9–11)—Anacardium, Nat. sulph., Aconite, Calc. fluor., Gelsemium, Kali phos., Phosphorus, Calc. sulph., Silica.

Pleura (9–11)—Bryonia, Cadmium sulph., Ant. crud., Calc. phos., Calc. sulph., Nat. phos., Aurum mur.

Bronchi (7–11)—Rumex, Bryonia, Calc. phos., Phosphorus, Nat. sulph., Aconite, Ferrum phos., Nat. mur., Kali phos.

Lungs (9–11)—Aconite lycot., Bryonia, Calc. phos., Nat. mur., Silica, Rumex.

Oesophagus (7–9)—Calc. fluor., Ruta, Symphytum, Calc. carb., Ferrum phos., Kali carb., Kali phos., Calc. phos., Causticum, Elaps cor., Euphorbium, Graphites, Lachesis.

Stomach (7–10)—Anacardium, Bismuth, Ipecac., Kali carb., Magn. phos., Nux vomica, Ornithogalum, Chamomilla.

Pylorus (6–12)—Sepia, Lycopodium, Graphites, Kali sulph., Nat. sulph., Calc. sulph., Lachesis, Nux vomica, Ornithogalum, Actaea rac., Card. mar., Calc. phos.

Gall bladder (7–9)—Calculus, Chelidonium, Calc. phos., Lycopodium, Thlaspi, Berberis, Calc. fluor., Helonias, Kali mur.

Liver (8–11)—Anacardium, Berberis, Lycopodium, Sulphur, Ferrum phos., Bryonia, Chelidonium, Colchicum, Crotalus, Hydrastis, Opium, Kali mur., Nux vomica, Podophyllum.

Spleen (7–10)—Arnica, Ceanothus, Chelidonium, Crotalus, Elaps cor., Ferrum phos., Lycopodium, Calc. sulph., Hydrastis, Lachesis, Nat. phos.

Kidney (7–9)—Erbium, Berberis, Lycopodium, Aconite, Apis, Cantharides, Erigeron, Hydrastis.

Pancreas (8–12)—Ferrum phos., Card. mar., Berberis, Iris flor., Kali sulph., Lycopodium, Nat. sulph., Ornithogalum, Capsicum, Iris v., Kali phos., Nat. sulph.

Duodenum (9–11)—Calc. fluor., Causticum, Kali sulph., Symphytum, Eupatorium, Ipecac., Kali carb., Ornithog., Ruta, Podophyllum, Pulsatilla.

Small intestine (8–11)—Anacardium, Ipecac., Sulphur, Arsenic alb., Lobelia erinus, Opium, Lobelia inflata, Lycopodium.

Caecum (7–12)—Crotalus, Dioscorea, Echinacea, Hepar sulph., Kali carb., Lachesis, Lycopodium, Elaps cor., Ignatia, Kali sulph., Nat. phos., Baptisia, Belladonna, Calc. phos. Graphites, Hydrastis, Sabadilla, Vipera, Calc. fluor.

Appendix (8–11)—Chamomilla, Lachesis, Nux vomica, Sulphur, Vipera, Belladonna, Cuprum, Hepar sulph., Hydrastis, Kali carb., Lycopodium, Aconite lycot., Calc. sulph., Elaps cor., Eupatorium, Ferrum phos., Kali mur., Magn. phos.

Colon (8–12)—Lycopodium, Sulphur, Calc. phos., Card mar., Lobelia erinus, Lobelia inflata, Hydrastis, Opium.

Bladder (8–10)—Petroleum, Staphisagria, Belladonna, Arsenic alb., Berberis, Cantharides, Formica.

Rectum (8–10)—Aesculus, Calc. sulph., Collinsonia, Hamamelis, Sulphur, Arnica, Causticum, Kali mur., Lycopodium, Ruta, Baptisia, Nux vomica, Podophyllum, Silica.

Bone (7–11)—Calc. carb., Silica, Arnica, Calc. fluor., Causticum, Eupatorium, Euphorbium, Aurum mur., Lycopodium, Mezereum, Ruta, Symphytum, Aurum met.

Skin (7–12)—Hepar sulph., Rhus tox, Sepia, Ignatia, Sulphur, Calc. carb., Formica, Graphites, Kali mur., Arsenic alb., Calc. sulph., Crotalus, Eupatorium, Silica, Stannum met., Vipera, Hydrastis, Lachesis, Nat. sulph., Platinum, Kali sulph., Magn. phos., Nat. mur.

Spinal cord (9–11)—Aconite, Calc. phos., Causticum, Coffea, Gelsemium, Ledum, Nat. mur., Tellurium, Calc. carb., Equisetum, Silica.

Spinal marrow (7–9)—Calc. phos., Eupatorium, Euphorbium, Lycopodium, Arnica, Calc. carb., Nat. mur., Nat. phos., Ruta,

Silica, Baryta carb., Causticum, Ferrum met., Sepia, Strychnine, Sulphur.

Cerebral substance (7–9)—Gelsemium, Kali carb., Argent. nit., Arnica, Calc. fluor., Calc. sulph., Nux vomica, Sepia, Baryta mur., Kali mur., Kali phos., Kali sulph., Magn. phos., Strychnine.

Sciatic nerve (6–9)—Capsicum, Actaea rac., Juglans regia, Magn. phos., Calc. phos., Eupatorium, Gelsemium, Kali phos., Calc. carb., Ferrum phos., Nat. phos., Rhus tox., Silica, Sulphur.

Grey matter (5–9)—Baryta mur., Baryta carb., Arnica, Eupatorium, Euphorbium, Kali phos., Lycopodium, Calc. fluor., Calc. sulph., Ferrum met., Ignatia, Kali sulph., Nat. sulph., Silica, Sulphur, Belladonna, Calc. phos., Causticum, Hypericum, Nat. mur., Phosphorus, Rhus tox.

Uterus (6–12)—Caulophyllum, Sepia, Aconite, Hydrastis, Lilium tigrum, Murex, Kali carb., Euphorbium Gelsemium, Ruta, Ignatia, Terebinth.

Ovary (7–12)—Fraxinus Americanus, Mentha pulegium, Aconite, Lilium tigrum, Sepia, Kali carb., Ruta, Murex, Calc. phos., Gelsemium.

Testicle (5–10)—Samarium, Lycopodium, Calc. phos., Silica, Aconite, Calc. carb., Calc. fluorica, Nat. sulph., Kali carb., Gelsemium.

Prostate (7–9)—Agnus castus, Belladonna, Caladium, Calc. carb., Sabadilla, Samarium, Selenium, Gelsemium.

Veins (5–9)—Arnica, Cactus, Anacardium, Baryta mur., Secale, Pulsatilla, Ferrum met., Ferrum phos., Kali phos.

Arteries (6–10)—Arnica, Baryta mur., Cactus, Pulsatilla, Aconite, Anacardium, Ferrum met., Ferrum phos., Secale, Arsenic alb., Kali carb., Gelsemium, Ruta.

Arteriosclerosis (7–10)—Anacardium, Argent nit., Arnica, Aurum met., Baryta mur., Calc. fluorica, Plumbum iod., Ferrum mur., Zincum, Ferrum met., Baryta carb.

I prepared a separate table for endocrine glands and their remedies, using compressed gland tablets and 6c remedies. As with the table for organs, the endocrines were tested on the P polarity. In this case the actual readings are given for each gland; the lower the reading, the closer is the affinity between gland and remedy.

It is obvious that the results do depend on the purity of the gland preparations. Although the samples used were not fresh, I do not think they had deteriorated in any way radiesthetically. It is indeed remarkable how a substance retains its radiesthetic influence over the years. Some of the results confirmed my faith in the method. For instance Samarium is perhaps *the* remedy for stimulating orchitic, and this came out very well on test. It will be noticed how well Gelsemium, Ledum and Lycopodium were indicated for suprarenal (whole gland). I was impressed by the fact that Arnica came out best for stimulating adrenalin. One might have supposed that the results for adrenalin and suprarenal medulla (as one specimen was labelled) would have been very similar. They do vary quite considerably and I have given the results as I recorded them. I included cortisone as the appertaining remedies might conceivably be useful for prescribing as alternative to the employment of cortisone itself.

TABLE II

Endocrine glands and their remedies

Pituitary (whole gland)—Aconite 9, Calc. phos 6, Dioscorea 8, Ferrum phos 6, Gelsemium 8, Kali iod 9, Kali mur 9, Kali phos 8, Silica 9.

Anterior pituitary—Calc. carb 8, Eupatorium 8, Kali sulph 9, Kalmia 9, Lycopodium 8, Nat. phos 8, Nat. sulph 9, Silica 9, Zincum 8.

Posterior pituitary—Agnus castus 7, Arnica 8, Baryta mur 9, Calc. carb 8, Calc. phos 8, Eupatorium 9, Phytolacca 8, Silica 9.

Pineal—Aurum sulph 9, Baryta carb 7, Bromium 8, Calc. fluorica 9, Equisetum 7, Indium 9, Iridium 8, Sepia 7.

Thymus—Aconite 9, Actaea rac 8, Baryta carb 7, Calc. carb 9, Calc. fluorica 6, Calc. phos 7, Equisetum 7, Eupatorium 8, Ferrum phos 8, Gelsemium 7, Kali carb 9, Kali mur 7, Kali phos 8, Kali sulph 9, Sabadilla 9.

Thyroid—Arsenic alb 9, Arsenic iod 8, Calc. carb 10, Equisetum 10, Eupatorium 9, Euphorbium 8, Graphites 10, Kali carb 7, Kali phos 8, Magnesium phos 10, Xanthox. 10.

Parathyroid—Baryta carb 10, Baryta mur 8, Calc. carb 9, Equisetum 8, Gelsemium 10, Iris v. 10, Kali carb 8, Kali mur 8, Kali sulph 9, Nat. mur 10, Vanadium 9.

Orchitic—Caladium 9, Calc. carb 9, Calc. fluorica 9, Kali carb 9, Ferrum phos 8, Kali sulph 9, Lycopodium 7, Magnesium phos 7, Nat mur 8, Nat. sulph 7, Samarium 6, Silica 9.

Ovarian—Aconite 8, Calc. phos 9, Helonias 9, Kali carb 9, Kali mur 8, Kali phos 9, Lilium tigrum 8, Magnesium phos 7, Mentha pulegium 8, Nat. sulph 7, Sepia 8, Silica 7.

Mammary—Actaea rac 8, Belladonna 8, Calc. fluorica 7, Helonias 10, Kali mur 10.

Suprarenal (whole gland)—Capsicum 8, Euphorbium 7, Gelsemium 6, Ledum 7, Lobelia erinata 8, Lobelia inflata 8, Lycopodium 7.

Suprarenal medulla—Argent met 7, Arnica 9, Aurum met 9, Calc. carb 8, Causticum 9, Ledum 9, Lobelia erinata 8.

Suprarenal cortex—Actaea rac 6, Arnica 8, Calc. carb 9, Causticum 9, Dioscorea 6, Eupatorium 9, Euphorbium 7, Iris flor 8, Lycopodium 7, Phosphorus 9.

Adrenalin—Arnica 7, Calc. phos 9, Ferrum phos 9, Gelsemium 8, Kali mur 8, Ledum 9, Lycopodium 9, Nat. sulph 9, Sabadilla 8.

Cortisone—Actaea rac 9, Ant. arsenic 7, Argent nit 7, Chin. arsenic 5, Chin. sulph 9, Hepar sulph 9, Kali phos 9, Sepia 7, Tellurium 9.

The standard list of Turenne organ witnesses includes a witness for arteriosclerosis, and so this is included in Table I, tested in exactly the same way as the other witnesses on the P polarity. In choosing remedies to test, I naturally looked for those which by their symptomatology might be expected to give good readings, and I was more concerned to test the common remedies in more universal use. At the same time I have on occasion gone out of my way to test rarer remedies, either because their action was known to me or because they appeared in one or other standard repertory. Remedies were also sometimes suggested to me by tables prepared by the late Dr. Guyon Richards and by Dr. H. Tomlinson. This applied especially to Table II.

Choosing remedies and testing them in the preparation of the tables was a lengthy business and there must be not a few remedies which could, or should, have been included in them. Practitioners can of course add to them as they think fit. Because a remedy is not there does not necessarily mean it is not suitable for toning up a particular organ or gland, always provided that it comes out well on test in any particular case. As with the nosodes, every organ and gland was tested with the twelve Schüssler salts.

In dealing with a case, only one or two remedies listed may be appropriate for toning up an organ. Indeed the best remedy may not be in the list at all. Due regard must be paid to the symptomatology of a remedy under consideration and how it measures up on the witness of the patient. It will also be understood that the method of test paid no regard to the magnetic balance of an organ as found in a patient and on which the tables of Drs. Richards and Tomlinson are based. My object was to find a physical relationship between organ and remedy quite independently of any consideration of the condition of a patient.

I can only say that I hope the tables may prove useful. In treating a patient, remedies required will often be determined more by infections to which he is subject than anything else. At the same time, when an organ or gland is diseased or in poor function, it may be necessary to find a remedy to deal specifically with it. For this purpose I think myself that 3x remedies can often be used with advantage (at the tissue level) to deal with the organ, together with whatever remedies are required in higher potency. These low potencies are particularly useful for toning up organs of the alimentary tract, and can assist higher potencies in clearing up infections with their accompanying toxaemia. Indeed for dealing with toxaemia as such, 3x remedies are very useful and can be tested on rates such as those for toxic condition, septicaemia, toxins, poisons and so on.

Chapter 15

Endocrine Glands and Vitamins

My object in this chapter is to show relationships between the endocrine glands, how they react on each other, and the effect of vitamins on endocrine activity. After making a whole series of tests, I came to the conclusion that the best way of testing out endocrine function was by means of the P polarity. My pure samples of the various endocrines consisted of compressed gland tablets.

I first placed Pineal ϕ on the rule at 0cm. with P on one side of it on a rubber block, which gave a P polarity reading of 23. I then placed Pineal 6 on the other side on another rubber block, which brought the reading down to 12. On the other hand Thymus 6 sent the reading up to 29. The following are the results I obtained, arranging the glands in pairs, using pure gland samples and 6c potencies.

Tests of glands on P polarity

Pineal ϕ	23		Thymus ϕ	23
With Pineal 6	12		With Thymus 6	12
With Thymus 6	29		With Pineal 6	28
Anterior pituitary ϕ	23		Post. pituitary ϕ	23
With Ant. pituitary 6	13		With Post. pituitary 6	12
With Post. pituitary 6	28		With Ant. pituitary 6	28
Thyroid ϕ	23		Parathyroid ϕ	23
With Thyroid 6	11		With Parathyroid 6	15
With Parathyroid 6	16		With Thyroid 6	17
Orchitic ϕ	23		Ovarian ϕ	22
With Orchitic 6	11		With Ovarian 6	11
With Ovarian 6	12		With Orchitic 6	11
Suprarenal cortex ϕ	22		Suprarenal medulla ϕ	23
With S. cortex 6	11		With S. medulla 6	11
With S. medulla 6	17		With S. cortex 6	16

The glands are paired in such a way that they might be supposed to have some related function, or that they occur anatomically in juxtaposition. It would seem natural, for instance, to find a relationship between the anterior and posterior pituitary glands, and equally natural to compare thyroid with parathyroid.

We know that in testing a patient on the P polarity with his specimen at 0cm., a remedy which suits him and provides a stimulus to his system will give a low reading, probably below 10cm. In a similar manner a gland, which will add to the activity of another gland, will also give a low reading when tested on the P polarity. Nothing will activate an organic substance better than a potency of itself, and it is for this reason that I tested each gland with a potency of itself.

An examination of the table reveals that in the case of pineal and thymus and of anterior pituitary and posterior pituitary, the paired gland in potency produced a relatively high reading, a good deal higher than the P polarity reading for the gland under test. I concluded from these readings that pineal and thymus antidoted each other's action, as did anterior and posterior pituitary.

In his book, *The Chain of Life*, Dr. Richards devoted some space to the action of pineal and thymus. Pineal is a stimulator, while thymus has a damping down, or sedative, effect. Richards used at times to prescribe Pineal gr. $\frac{1}{10}$ and I can testify to the strong tonic effect this can have. 'Thymus,' Richards said, 'should be given in cases where there is general over-activity of the metabolism and where any gland is overactive.' Both glands can be deficient and I recall that Argent nit is a remedy which can deal with this condition.

We can refer to pineal and thymus and anterior and posterior pituitary respectively as 'balancing glands'. If one gland is overactive, its pair may be under-active. But both could be deficient in function. It is evident that over-active anterior pituitary could be corrected by the administration of posterior-pituitary or a related remedy, if the posterior pituitary gland was not fully active itself.

A way of confirming the balancing effect of these two pairs of glands can be accomplished quite simply in the following manner. To take an actual example, that of a young and active man whose P polarity measured 35. Pineal 6 tested on his P polarity reduced the reading to 27, but the addition of Thymus 6 on the rubber block alongside Pineal 6 brought the reading back to 35. Anterior pituary 6 brought the reading down to 23, which was restored to 35 by the addition of posterior pituitary 6. On the other hand Thyroid 6 reduced his reading to 25, while adding Parathyroid 6 raised it to only 29. Orchitic 6 reduced the P polarity reading to 25, a reading which the addition of Ovarian 6 did not alter.

In the case of thyroid and parathyroid, from the readings in the table I concluded that these two glands are not linked together as balancing glands, although we know that while thyroid is a stimulator, the action of parathyroid is sedative. Their functions are, of course, quite separate. From the table it would appear that the stimulating effect of the potentised female sex gland on the male is very much the same as that of the potentised male gland, and vice versa. It must be understood that in such tests we are considering only the effect of one gland on another, which is not the same thing as when we consider the effect of glandular action in a patient, which will depend on the totality of his electrical or dynamic balance, including the balancing forces of his whole endocrine system.

The task I next set myself was to find what effect endocrines generally have on the sex glands. Again I employed the P polarity system, which appeared to give the most consistent results. In other words, it was easier to obtain precise balance points than by other methods tested. The results were as follows:

Sex glands tested on P polarity

Orchitic ϕ	23	Ovarian ϕ		23
With Pineal 6	11	With Pineal 6		11
With Thymus 6	14	With Thymus 6		26
With Ant. pituitary 6	11	With Ant. pituitary 6		27
With Post. pituitary 6	25	With Post. pituitary 6		11
With Thyroid 6	10	With Thyroid 6		11
With Parathyroid 6	11	With Parathyroid 6		11
With S. cortex 6	15	With S. cortex 6		15
With S. medulla 6	15	With S. medulla 6		15
With Mammary 6	16	With Mammary 6		10

It will be seen from this table that pineal, anterior pituitary, thyroid and parathyroid were the main stimulators of orchitic, while pineal, posterior pituitary, thyroid, parathyroid and mammary were the main stimulators of ovarian. As we previously found, orchitic and ovarian are mutual stimulators of each other. On the other hand, according to the readings, posterior pituitary would appear to inhibit orchitic secretion and thymus and anterior pituitary that of ovarian.

It is interesting to compare these results with those obtained by Guyon Richards as recorded in the section on sex glands in *The Chain of Life*. One marked difference is that, according to Richards, parathyroid decreased both orchitic and ovarian activity. In getting out a table of this kind, one finds that some readings come out more positively than others. The strength of the influence appears to be

I

stronger, so that one arrives at the balance point more easily. In some tests the pendulum appears to 'wander' over a spread of 3 or 4cm., and one can sometimes find the true balance point best by taking the mean of the two extreme readings. In the present case, it was very obvious in handling the pendulum how the anterior and posterior principles of the pituitary gland stimulate the male and female sex glands respectively. To me it is remarkable that we can obtain results like this at all when dealing with 'dead' matter, which is a very different proposition to testing endocrine function in a live human being.

It is not for me to assess the value of these readings. A great deal of work has been done in the field of endocrinology and all that I have attempted to show is possible ways in which radiesthesia might add something to the already extensive knowledge which we already have. If this method is viable, and I think it is, it provides a quick and ready way of testing out the action of various substances on the endocrine glands, including the glands themselves. My hope is that others will follow up researches on similar lines.

Again using the P polarity method I thought it might be of interest to test out endocrines on mammary gland. These were the results:

Mammary gland tested on P polarity

Mammary ϕ	22
With Pineal 6	12
With Thymus 6	11
With Pituitary 6 (whole gland)	14
With Ant. pituitary 6	16
With Post. pituitary 6	16
With Thyroid 6	16
With Parathyroid 6	16
With Orchitic 6	23
With Ovarian 6	10
With Suprarenal 6 (whole gland)	21
With S. cortex 6	23
With S. medulla 6	23
With Cortisone 6	27

Pineal, thymus and ovarian all appear to have a strongly stimulating effect on mammary secretion. But what is possibly the most interesting result in the table is the inhibitory effect of Cortisone.

Turning to the action of vitamins on endocrine activity, I used two methods, the P polarity method and the employment of 6c potencies. In the latter case I put a 6c potency of the gland at 0cm.

on the rule and each 6c potentised vitamin in radiative contact with it (on a rubber block alongside the 0cm. mark). It is interesting to compare results obtained by both methods.

Effect of vitamins on endocrines

Thyroid on P polarity		Thyroid using 6c's only	
Thyroid ϕ	23/24	Thyroid 6	32
With Vitamin A 6	18	With Vitamin A 6	26
With Vitamin B 6	21	With Vitamin B 6	26
With Vitamin C 6	19	With Vitamin C 6	28
With Vitamin D 6	23	With Vitamin D 6	26
With Vitamin E 6	24	With Vitamin E 6	26
With Vitamin B12 6	22	With Calcarea carb. 6	21
With Calcarea carb. 6	17	With Iodum 6	26
With Iodum 6	20		

Parathyroid on P polarity		Parathyroid using 6c's only	
Parathyroid ϕ	23/24	Parathyroid 6	32
With Vitamin A 6	23	With Vitamin A 6	25
With Vitamin B 6	24	With Vitamin B 6	25
With Vitamin C 6	21	With Vitamin C 6	28
With Vitamin D 6	19	With Vitamin D 6	25
With Vitamin E 6	23	With Vitamin E 6	26
With Vitamin B12 6	22	With Vitamin B12 6	22
With Calcarea carb. 6	17	With Calcarea carb. 6	18
With Iodum 6	21	With Iodum 6	28

Orchitic on P polarity		Orchitic using 6c's only	
Orchitic ϕ	23/24	Orchitic 6	31
With Vitamin A 6	20	With Vitamin A 6	20
With Vitamin B 6	21	With Vitamin B 6	20
With Vitamin C 6	22	With Vitamin C 6	19
With Vitamin D 6	19	With Vitamin D 6	15
With Vitamin E 6	15	With Vitamin E 6	12
With Vitamin B12 6	20	With Vitamin B12 6	15

Ovarian on P polarity		Ovarian using 6c's only	
Ovarian ϕ	23/24	Ovarian 6	32
With Vitamin A 6	21	With Vitamin A 6	20
With Vitamin B 6	21	With Vitamin B 6	20
With Vitamin C 6	21	With Vitamin C 6	17
With Vitamin D 6	19	With Vitamin D 6	18
With Vitamin E 6	19	With Vitamin E 6	10
With Vitamin B12 6	20	With Vitamin B12 6	12

Mammary on P polarity	
Mammary ϕ	23/24
With Vitamin A 6	21
With Vitamin B 6	20
With Vitamin C 6	19
With Vitamin D 6	19
With Vitamin E 6	16
With Vitamin B12 6	17

Mammary using 6c's only	
Mammary 6	30
With Vitamin A 6	20
With Vitamin B 6	18
With Vitamin C 6	16
With Vitamin D 6	18
With Vitamin E 6	10
With Vitamin B12 6	12

Suprarenal cortex on P polarity	
Suprarenal cortex ϕ	23/24
With Vitamin A 6	21
With Vitamin B 6	19
With Vitamin C 6	19
With Vitamin D 6	21
With Vitamin E 6	23
With Vitamin B12 6	21

Suprarenal cortex using 6c's only	
Suprarenal cortex 6	29
With Vitamin A 6	20
With Vitamin B 6	20
With Vitamin C 6	18
With Vitamin D 6	20
With Vitamin E 6	27
With Vitamin B12 6	21

Suprarenal medulla on P polarity	
Suprarenal medulla ϕ	23/24
With Vitamin A 6	24
With Vitamin B 6	23
With Vitamin C 6	21
With Vitamin D 6	24
With Vitamin E 6	23
With Vitamin B12 6	23

Adrenalin using 6c's only	
Adrenalin 6	31
With Vitamin A 6	25
With Vitamin B 6	18
With Vitamin C 6	15
With Vitamin D 6	20
With Vitamin E 6	18
With Vitamin B12 6	17

The method using 6c potencies is analogous to the method employed for comparing the action of drugs on nosodes, only in the latter case 30c potencies were used. As iodine is such an important constituent of the thyroid gland and calcium of the parathyroid, thyroid and parathyroid were tested with Calcarea carb. and Iodum. It is to be observed that Calcarea carb. gave the lowest reading in all four group tests, from which we might infer that calcium is as important in thyroid function as it is for parathyroid. Clinically it is often wanted to increase thyroid secretion, just as it is for parathyroid.

In these tests results appear to be better when testing with the '6c's only' method. This may be due to the much stronger radiesthetic influence of a 6c potency as compared with compressed gland preparations, which incidentally had been in my possession for some considerable time. So I think the proper approach to the table is to take the '6c's only' group tests as the primary ones, to be compared and checked against the *P* polarity group tests. The readings represent one set of tests only. If one tries to check up on a reading which appears to be faulty, auto-suggestion can so easily creep into checked results. Also a difficulty that arises is that at different times all readings may be slightly greater or less than the original ones. This may well be due to atmospheric conditions, applied in the widest sense. However it is the *relative* readings in any one group test that matter, and on the whole these were fairly consistent.

I have commented at some length on these tests so as to underline the advantages and limitations of the radiesthetic method. In extended research work in a laboratory it would be necessary to have a planned programme of repetitive tests, carried out preferably by two or more radiesthetists. It is always open to the radiesthetist to try to find a method providing greater consistency in the results.

To revert to the table. Apart from Calcarea carb., Vitamin D appears to be the most important vitamin in parathyroid function when we compare the two methods, which again is not surprising in view of the fact that Vitamin D is required for the proper assimilation of calcium. It certainly shows up well on the *P* polarity test. It may be of some interest that taking the tests with 6c potencies only, the addition of Vitamin D 6 to Calcarea carb. 6 on the rubber block brought the reading down from 18 to 9!

Coming to the sex glands and including mammary gland, the readings confirm the importance of Vitamin E for the proper function of these glands. By the '6c's only' method, Vitamin B12 comes out very well. Vitamin D also comes out well for stimulating orchitic. There is nothing remarkable about vitamin action on suprarenal cortex, except perhaps to observe that Vitamin E is possibly an antidote, if given in excess. With regard to suprarenal medulla ϕ (the tablets were actually labelled thus) and tests on Adrenalin 6, Vitamin C would appear to be of greatest importance among the vitamins in keeping this gland active. I believe this corresponds with the clinical findings of practitioners. I have not included tests on pineal and thymus and the pituitaries for the sake of brevity, but in any case they showed little by way of interesting variations as tested on the *P* polarity.

We know that some vitamins can complement each other and go very well together. Two such vitamins are A and D. I tested out the interaction of the vitamins, using the '6c's only' method, with the following results:

Interaction of vitamins

Vitamin A 6	32	Vitamin C 6	32
With Vitamin B 6	27	With Vitamin B 6	18
With Vitamin C 6	17	With Vitamin D 6	21
With Vitamin D 6	17	With Vitamin E 6	14
With Vitamin E 6	17	With Vitamin B12 6	14
With Vitamin B12 6	25		
Vitamin D 6	32	Vitamin E 6	32
With Vitamin B 6	20	With Vitamin B 6	17
With Vitamin E 6	14	With Vitamin B12 6	15
With Vitamin B12 6	17		
Vitamin B 6	32		
With Vitamin B12 6	14		

From the table, while Vitamin A complements C, D and E, C and E go very well together, but C and D not so well. Also D complements E. So we might say that a composite preparation of A, D and E is better in theory without the addition of C. Where Vitamin E is prescribed to prevent a miscarriage, the addition of Vitamin D should be well worth while. According to the table Vitamin C complements Vitamin B12, as also Vitamin E. Vitamin B12 complements Vitamin E, and B12, C and E should all go well together. Not surprisingly, Vitamins B and B12 are fully complementary.

It should be understood that where several vitamins are given to a patient, they will all benefit him if his system is deficient in them, whether they are strictly complementary or not. But where two vitamins are antagonistic to each other, as for instance Vitamins A and B, or A and B12, it would at least in theory be better to avoid giving them together to a patient unless he is known to be deficient in both. It is probably only in intensive vitamin treatment where considerations of this kind could usefully apply.

Chapter 16

Miscellaneous Procedures

I have explained how putting up the rate for inflammation of an organ provides a measure of the organ's toxicity. This is correct, but at the same time inflammation is not quite the same thing as toxaemia. I have also explained how the nosode Septicaemin 30 can be employed in conjunction with the rule for indicating toxicity. We can use the rate for an organ such as the stomach, which is 32, which may give a reading of, say, 48 or 49, indicating normal function. If it measured 46 or 47, it would not be fully active. On the other hand, if it measured 50, this might very well be an indication that it was slightly overactive (with a reading over 50 it would definitely be so), due to some infection. If we brought Septicaemin 30 in radiative contact with the witness of the organ at 100cm., which might be a Turenne witness, an animal organ preserved in alcohol or the waveform of the organ provided by a radionic instrument in conjunction with the vial connection, the reading might very well go up to 60. That would be a measure of the organ's toxicity.

We could of course put up the rate for inflammation of the stomach, which would probably show a reading like 55cm. Using Septicaemin 30 adjacent to the 100cm. mark might easily take the reading up to 60, or more. Again this would be a measure of the organ's toxicity, although inflammation set on the instrument in front of an organ rate also gives a measure of toxicity.

We could put up the Delawarr rate for toxic condition, which is 90222, and add to it the rate for stomach. This, however, would not give quite such a good idea of the state of the organ because it is represented by the fifth and sixth tuning dials. Where two combined rates are used, the further the second rate appears in the sequence of the dials from the first rate, which is the disease rate, the less influence it has in shaping the character of the combined waveform produced in the instrument by the two rates. It is for this reason that the rate for inflammation of the stomach gives a better idea of the condition of the stomach than the combined rate for toxic condition of the stomach. The shorter the first rate, the greater the impact of the second rate in its representation in the combined waveform. An advantage of the Drown rate for toxic condition, which is 6065, might be said to be its use of only three dials. All this should help the reader to appreciate the value of the rate for inflammation, represented by one dial only.

Persons using radionic instruments may at times want to find a rate for a nosode, which is the potency of a pathogenic organism developed from a culture medium. To show how this can be done, let us take the nosode of B. coli 30. We place the sample at 0cm. on the rule with the vial connection-cum-instrument at the 100cm. mark. All the dials on the instrument are set at 0 except the last one, the measuring dial, which is set at 8. We then obtain a reading of about 30 on the rule. Next we turn the first dial to 10 (remembering that we are dealing with a disease condition) and we find that the balance point has gone up to about 40cm. With the first dial at 20, and then at 30, the reading will go up further. But if we turn the dial to 40, the rule balance point will go down. The first two digits in our rate are thus 30. We start in exactly the same way with dial 2 and find that the correct setting for the B coli nosode is 2. Turning dial 3, at no point does the reading increase. Thus our rate for B. coli is 3020.

We can check this rate in the following manner. With only the sample of B. Coli 30 at 0cm. on the rule, we bring another vial connection arrangement into radiative contact with it, i.e. we place one vial alongside the 0cm. mark of the rule on a rubber block with the second vial on the instrument. We could use the same instrument for operations at both ends of the rule, but it is more convenient to employ two instruments, an additional advantage being that their accuracy can be checked against each other.

Now, with all the dials on the instrument at 0 except perhaps the last, which may be set at 8 (actually I think it makes little difference in this case whether this dial is set at 8 or left at 0), we shall get a balance point on the rule of something like 30cm. If we now set up the complementary rate of 3020, which is 7080, on the instrument, we find that the balance point is 10cm. or below. Thus the complementary rate practically cuts out the waveform of the nosode, thus confirming the correct finding of the recognition rate.

Sometimes it is difficult, or indeed impossible, to obtain a rate by the first method with the vial connection at 100cm. This really does not matter, as greater precision in finding a rate is secured by the second method, with the vial connection at 0cm. In fact, often enough it is difficult to determine by the first method what the last figure should be in, say, a four-figure rate. This can easily be found by the second method because, having set up the complementary rate, turning the third dial a division up or down will indicate which rate will produce the lowest reading. As a rule it should be possible to get a reading of, say, 8cm. If we are finding a rate for an organism and this is not attainable with the three dials, we can proceed to use the fourth, and so on, until we obtain a rate which effectively cuts out the nosode's waveform.

The Delawarr rate for B. Coli is 3017, which should be accepted as the standard rate. This does not mean that the rate for my nosode of 3020 was wrong. Actually there is very little difference between them and we cannot expect that samples of any particular organism would always produce exactly the same rate, however carefully they were prepared. Moreover, slightly different strains of one type of virus or bacterium may present themselves, and we must realise that the rates do provide a means of very close tuning.

For my nosode of Asian influenza I obtained a rate of 3033. With the vial connection opposite 0cm. on the rule, the complement of this brought the reading down to 10. The complement of the Delwarr rate of 30238 for this infection also brought the reading down to 10, but with the vial connection at 100cm. my rate of 3033 produced a reading of 50, whereas the Delawarr rate produced one of 45. So my rate was a more accurate rate for the nosode under test. Actually it will be appreciated that there was very little in it either way.

Some miscellaneous rates for nosodes tested are as follows:

Enterococcus	5012	Influenza Asian	3033
Faecalis alkaligenes (Bach)	5020	Influenza Spanish	3032
Morgan-Gaertner(Paterson)	3040	B. influenzae	30252
Mutabile	5033	Haem. influenzae	4071
Staph. abdominalis	3073	Asceptic meningitis	2034
Staph. haem. aureus	3014	Bronchisepticus	8021
Staph. pyogenes	3023	Cornybacterium coryzae	50423
Calf diptheria	20329	Micrococcus catarrhalis	5024
T.A.B.C.	7022	Koch-Weeks	7040
Pyrogen (pus)	4024	Morax-Axenfeldt	1040
		Mucobacter	40578

Tuberculins

Tuberculinum	60229
T.B. Bovinum	8098
T.B. Koch	2034
Denys	4043
Marmorek	20322
T.B. Meningitis	3030
Sycotic	7007

Where a disease rate begins with the digits 50, which is a cancer rate, the complement is taken not as 50, but as 90. Vindication of this is seen in the rate of 5024 for Micrococcus catarrhalis. Taking the complement of this rate as 9086 with the vial connection at 0cm., a reading of 6 was secured, which effectively cuts out the nosode's waveform. Where practitioners employ the recognition rate of an organism for broadcast treatment, the action must be to stimulate the organism to the point of disruption. But any micro-organisms which survived the treatment might become to that extent more virulent and also more resistant. The series of tests just des-cribed, which any competent radiesthetist could carry out, can in my opinion be taken as proof of the validity and effectiveness of the complementary rates, which have been used by many practitioners in the past with very good results.

Supposing that one has a nosode of whose origin one is uncertain. Such a one might be Sycotic. Sycosis has been defined as the gonorrhoeal toxin, but from what I had read, I thought that the nosode in my possession labelled 'Sycotic 30' might represent tubercular toxins. I proceeded to find out what I could about the nosode by means of a simple radiesthetic test.

I placed my sample of Sycotic 30 at 0cm. on my rule and put various other 30c nosodes in radiative contact with it, i.e. alongside it on a rubber block. I obtained an R reading of 31 for Sycotic 30, i.e. with nothing else on the rule or in radiative contact with the nosode. The readings with the other nosodes were as follows:

Sycotic 30 at 0cm.	31
With Gonorrhoea 30	25
With Medorrhinum 30	30
With Syphilinum 30	25
With Bacillinum 30	22
With Tuberculinum 30	22
With T.B. Bovinum 30	16
With T.B. Koch 30	16
With Denys 30	16
With Marmorek 30	16
With Streptococcus 30	31
With Psorinum 30	25
With Septicaemin 30	22

From these tests I concluded that my sample of Sycotic 30 referred pre-eminently to the tubercular strains.

I dealt in Chapter 9 at some length with the diagnosis and treat-ment of parasites and mentioned that I had several Turenne witnesses representing various parasitic infections. In most cases of parasitic infection I think they can be dealt with satisfactorily with the rates provided by the manufacturers of radionic instruments. But there may be occasions when the practitioner requires all the information he can collect concerning a case of parasites. Such a case came my way recently. It was of a lady who for the previous twenty years had suffered from a greasy skin and recurring skin eruptions. These were unsightly, but not irritable. When I first saw her I diagnosed mild parasitic infection. I dealt with this satisfactorily, as I thought, there being no signs afterwards of infestation of the intestinal tract, while on test the skin condition appeared to be much improved. However, my patient reported no change. Further tests revealed chicken-pox toxins and my patient told me that she had had a severe attack of chicken-pox when a girl, at about the same time that her skin became greasy. I cleared up these toxins only to be told that there was still no change. I treated the case with Natrum mur. (for greasy skin) without effect and with intensive vitamin treatment. Eventually, thinking there might be some obscure dysfunction of the endocrine glands, I tried to ensure that these were functioning normally. The administration of Calcarea carb. 6, which was very well indicated, brought the whole endocrine system into perfect balance and full function. But there was still nothing to report.

It was at this stage that I went back to extensive tests for parasites. On the triangle the Turenne witness for Taenia (pork) gave a reading of about 60–70°. When I added the witness of skin to the Taenia witness (both just inside the circle), I obtained a reading of 90° plus. I then worked out a rate for this taenia witness and made similar tests on the rule. The combined rate of Taenia into skin also produced a high reading on the rule. It was doubtless due to the fact that my patient was so well balanced up generally that the indication for taenia showed up so well on test. This is something which is familiar to radiesthetists.

It was on account of this case that I decided to procure rates for the Turenne witnesses for parasites in my possession, as they might come in useful, both for broadcast treatment and for microsonic therapy. These were the rates I obtained:

Taenia, beef	4028
Taenia, pork	3034
Trichinosis (infection caused by pork)	5003
Trichocephalus (a genus of parasitic worms)	30325
Botriocephalus (a genus of tape-worms)	30337
Anguilla (a genus of thread worms)	3022

Oxyuris (thread worm)   30339
Ascaris (roundworm)   40112
Ascaris Lumbricoides (roundworm)   4048
Actinomycosis (fungus)   4050

I worked out remedies to deal with these parasitic infections. They were all tested in 6c potency on the P polarity. In use they may be needed in 1x or 3x potency, in addition to higher potencies indicated. Worms represent a gross condition and can be highly toxic. Strong measures may be needed to eradicate them and we should remember Cuprum Oxy Nig. plus Antimony Crud. in this connection, very effective for tape-worm, which is generally prescribed in 1x potency. The range of readings is given in each case and the remedies appear with the better indicated appearing before those less well indicated. Those having the same reading appear in alphabetical order:

Taenia, beef (11–12)—Nat. sulph., Spigelia, Chenopodium, Dulcamara, Ignatia, Podophyllum, Tellurium.
Taenia, pork (8–12)—Nat. phos., Sabadilla, Calc. phos., Chenopodium, Cuprum, Granatum, Calc. carb. Ferrum phos., Podophyllum, Nat. mur., Nat. sulph., Sulphur, Tellurium.
Trichinosis (8–12)—Ignatia, Nat. phos., Sabadilla, Chenopodium, Cuprum, Magnesium phos., Nat. sulph., Calc. carb., Sepia.
Trichocephalus (11–12)—Calc. fluorica, Chenopodium, Kali sulph., Nat. mur., Nat. sulph., Calc. sulph., Dulcamara, Ferrum phos., Granatum, Ignatia, Pulsatilla, Rhus tox., Silica, Spigelia.
Botriocephalus (9–12)—Spigelia, Chenopodium, Ferrum phos., Nat. phos., Nat. sulph., Tellurium.
Anguilla (8–12)—Pulsatilla, Sabadilla, Kali phos., Calc. carb., Calc. fluorica, Cina, Calc. phos., Sulphur.
Oxyuris (7–12)—Ignatia, Nat. phos., Cina, Pulsatilla, Spigelia, Calc. carb., Calc. phos., Dulcamara, Kali mur., Graphites, Sabadilla, Sepia, Kali sulph., Lycopodium, Sulphur, Teucrium, Cuprum, Silica.
Ascaris (7–12)—Podophyllum, Sabadilla, Ignatia, Pulsatilla, Calc. fluorica, Lycopodium, Nat. mur., Sulphur, Tellurium, Nat. phos., Calc. carb., Chenopodium, Granatum, Nat. sulph., Sepia.
Ascaris Lumbricoides (8–12)—Calc. fluorica, Ignatia, Calc. carb., Spigelia, Cuprum, Granatum, Nat. sulph., Sabadilla, Tellurium, Cina, Kali mur., Magnesium phos., Nat. sulph., Sulphur.
Actinomycosis (9–12)—Chenopodium, Ant. crud., Calc. sulph., Dulcamara, Graphites, Lycopodium, Magnesium phos., Nat. mur., Pulsatilla, Sabadilla.

I decided to find rates for a few of the lesser-known Turenne organ witnesses. These are:

Blood, normal	4434
Red corpuscles	4463
White corpuscles	4510 (4 dials)
Pepsin	3551
Pelvis, bone structure	84077
Bone decalcification	40223

Where the digits 10 appear in a rate, it is usual to treat them as the number 10 to be set on one dial. However, with regard to white corpuscles, the rate obtained was on four dials with the digit 1 on the third and 0 on the fourth. As to the rate I obtained for normal blood, 4434, if I disconnected the vial connection at 100cm. and made one at 0cm. alongside the witness for normal blood, and then put up the complementary rate of 6676, I obtained a reading of 8. Thus the complementary rate cut out very effectively the waveform of normal blood, confirming the correctness of the recognition rate, viz. 4434. The Delawarr rate for blood is 409. By substituting the complementary rate of this, which is 601, for the complementary rate I obtained myself for blood, I still obtained a reading of 8 when tested against the Turenne witness. Thus one can only conclude that both rates are correct rates for blood and give a correct indication of normal blood, although they are different. This is proof enough to me that one can have more than one rate for one item. Whereas the Delawarr complementary rate of 601 provided a reading of 8 tested against the witness for normal blood, the rate 600 produced one of 23 and 602 one of 15. This shows how highly selective radionic instruments can be. Obviously the rate for the Turenne witness does not represent *exactly* the same substance as that represented by the Delawarr rate, but they both accurately represent blood, and the difference between them (whatever it is) is of minimal significance.

I have laboured this point at some length because one sometimes hears it argued that because different people get different rates for supposedly the same item, the rates have no objective value. The simple test just described, which any radiesthetist can repeat, constitutes to my mind just one reason why such a conclusion is wrong.

When testing an organ on the rule, we can test it on S and P (see p. 27) and with the rate for inflammation, which generally is associated with toxaemia. In the ordinary way when testing an organ on the rule, I place a sample of S alongside the organ specimen at the 100cm. mark, as already explained. This is really 'testing the organ on S', and if we want to test it on P, we replace S by P. Any difference between the readings for S and P indicates some 'magnetic'

imbalance in the organ, and as we already know, with the reading of
P higher than *S*, we can assume that the organ is being assailed by
some infection or other.

When dealing with highly sensitive or nervous patients, it may
help at times to test the sympathetic and parasympathetic nervous
systems (the Delawarr rates are 739 and 7510 respectively). These
may both give a reading of 49 or 50cm., but testing on *S* and *P*
may show some imbalance in the nervous system. It may be simpler,
however, to test for inflammation of the sympathetic and parasympathetic nervous systems respectively, which may show a positive
reading (over 45cm., according to my way of working). This really
represents an over-stimulation of the nervous system and can produce very unpleasant symptoms. And it could quite easily be due to
over-stimulation caused by remedies the patient has been taking,
constituting an overdose. This sort of reaction is more common in
patients of a nervous disposition. It could be caused through worry
or psychological factors. If it is purely a case of over-stimulation,
Natrum mur. may be the remedy to reduce the reading for inflammation to below 10cm., this being a good indication for its administration. Natrum mur. is an excellent remedy for tension of either a
mental or physical character.

Measurements of an organ on *S* and *P* can equally be made on
the triangle with *S* and *P* placed successively in radiative contact
with the organ witness, but just outside the circle. It can also be
tested with *S* and *P* placed successively at C. The Turenne standard
list of witnesses includes one for 'Great Sympathetic', i.e. the sympathetic nervous system. Without the assistance of Turenne witnesses,
samples of *S* and *P* themselves make quite good witnesses of the
twin balancing principles of the autonomic nervous system.

In helping delicate or run-down patients, a rate that can be useful
is 'inflammation of the suprarenal gland'. Secretion of this gland can
easily be affected through infection, which may be a leading factor in
complaints of weakness and debility by the patient. It may be desirable
to find a remedy to include in the prescription which reduces a
positive reading for this rate to 45cm. The gland can of course also be
tested on the rate for 'deficiency', which may show a positive reading.
If it does, the rate for suprarenal gland by itself, which is 8778, should
produce a reading signifiying lack of function, say anything below
47cm. A remedy that corrects this when tested against the patient's
specimen at 0cm. on the rule should restore the reading to 48–50cm.
We do know, however, that the best way of finding such a remedy
would be to test it on the 'deficiency' reading, which should take the
reading down to below 10cm. A similar reading could be expected if
the test were made on the rate for inflammation of the gland.

Chapter 17

Conclusion

The basic principle of homoeopathy is prescribing a remedy for a patient which would produce his symptoms in a normal healthy subject. It was Hahnemann who developed this idea, but being very much concerned with the methods of treatment of his day with large doses of harmful drugs and the widespread practice of vene-section, he decided to find out whether drugs given in quite small quantities could be effective. His researches in this direction proved highly successful, so much so that he experimented with drugs in minute quantities.

There must have come a point when, in order to carry his investigations further, he took one very small part of his already much diluted medicine and mixed it with a very much larger quantity of his neutral base. By repeating the process he prepared medicines in which the amount of the original drug was infinitesimal. But what some people do not seem to realise is that Hahnemann not only diluted his medicines, but potentised them. It is this potentisation of the homoeopathic remedy, more especially in the higher potencies, which confers on it its exceptional powers.

On more than one occasion medical men high up in their profession have told me in no uncertain terms that there is nothing of value in homoeopathy because the amount of drug employed is so very small that it can have no therapeutic effect. It is suggested that any effect that a remedy has must be psychological and due to the belief that the patient has in the treatment. People who talk like this are so wedded to the material aspect of medicine that any arguments as to the radiative properties of the homoeopathic remedy mean nothing to them. One has no point of contact with them.

Possibly it might help some readers if we were to compare the action of homoeopathic remedies with electricity. In electricity we have voltage and amperage, pressure and quantity of flow. To cause a spark between two electrodes, we may need quite a high voltage, depending on the nature of the electrodes and the size of the gap between them. It is the pressure, or voltage, which really matters, the quantity of flow being only secondary. But to provide heat from an electric fire, we need a comparatively large quantity of flow of electricity at a moderate pressure.

It is rather like that with homoeopathy. High potencies are like high voltages. They can have a deep and lasting effect on virulent disease, reducing its intensity (or voltage) to a point where lower potency remedies (nearer to the tissue level) can take over, and by their greater quantity of drug content (greater quantity of flow or amperage) act more directly on the diseased tissue.

If once we can accept the idea of energy levels in health and disease, the matter becomes simpler. I contend that homoeopathy does help one to understand the nature of disease. For in homoeopathy, as I have previously pointed out, we are matching the energy of the drug to the energy level, or virulence, of the disease. It should be easier for us to understand this today when we know that in physics there is no such thing as solid matter, but that everything consists of particles in violent motion. The high potency remedy, containing an infinitely small amount of the drug from which it was originally prepared, nevertheless retains the nature of the drug and transfers it to the patient, as it were, at high voltage. But it can only affect those attributes of the patient which themselves function at the same level of intensity. Thus it comes about that in dealing with mental cases, it is often the high potency which will benefit the patient. We would expect virus and bacterial infections to need lower potencies, say of the order of 6 and 30 and up to 200, while lower potencies still, such as 3x, may be required (in addition to whatever is necessary in higher potencies) to turn the scale in the treatment of diseased tissue.

If my readers have come with me thus far, they will appreciate that in dealing with these highly attenuated drug preparations, it is all important to prescribe not only the correct remedy, but the correct potency also. It is somewhat like tuning a wireless set. Unless one tunes in accurately to the station, the results are practically nil. On the other hand, the allopathic remedy can be said to have a wider field of action and to that extent favourable results of some sort may more easily accrue. But when we get our homoeopathic remedy right, both as to drug and potency, the results can be far-reaching. Moreover, the homoeopathic Materia Medica provides us with a choice of drugs and variety of treatment which gives the practitioner a scope in dealing with a case far exceeding anything that can be achieved in allopathy.

I must confess at this juncture that I have much sympathy with the medical men who deny the validity of homoeopathy. It has had too many failures in the past. Too often the practitioner, in tuning his wireless set, has missed the station. There is nothing wrong in theory with the classical method of homoeopathic prescribing, i.e. prescribing on symptoms, but in practice it is essential, in my opinion, if results are to attain an acceptable standard of success, to have some method of testing. There is nothing to be compared in classical homoeopathic prescribing with the precise testing, both as to choice of drug and potency, which is available to the radiesthetist.

As I have asserted earlier in this book, the treatment of diseased tissue may require remedies in low potency, i.e. homoeopathic remedies of which there is the widest possible choice. But it is impossible to choose these remedies correctly without some method of radiesthetic testing. It is only when we employ some method of testing that we can use low potency remedies repetitively as they ought to be used.

In conclusion, there is one point which it is necessary to stress. Whatever opinion the individual may have of the homoeopathic remedy, to deny that it can have any positive value is patently wrong. The reason is that most homoeopathic remedies are obtainable in quite low potencies, while some can be had in mother tincture (unpotentised). The best all-round low potency is probably 3x, which has a dilution of 1 in 1,000. For some drugs, such as the snake poisons, this is too low a potency for safe use. For such a drug as Arsenic alb., however, the concentration of drug in the 3x potency is sufficient for it to be labelled 'Poison'.

At one time there were what were known in homoeopathic circles as the high potency and low potency schools. I suppose they exist to some extent today. No one has to use high potencies, and the action of low potencies is to some extent comparable with that of allopathic drugs. For the radiesthetist, the answer is clear. He will choose his remedies and his potencies according to his tests. Homoeopaths know that for the treatment of a tape worm, or for that matter a hang-over, strong, crude, or low-potency, drugs are required. On the other hand they also know that something higher than 3x potencies will be needed to treat effectively an attack of influenza, even though low-potency remedies may be included in the treatment.

As a layman I have little knowledge of allopathic drugs and in my radiesthetic researches I have come to value the homoeopathic remedy at its true worth. But I must emphasise that the radiesthetic method is not restricted to homoeopathy. It could be employed by allopaths with equal advantage. I hope therefore that doctors generally and others engaged in one or other therapeutic field, will come to regard radiesthesia as a useful ally—one which becomes more valuable as acquaintance with it becomes closer.

Suggested Remedies

The tiro in radiesthesia wishing to take an interest in homoeopathy for the first time may wonder what remedies he should order for a start. I have chosen thirty remedies which should make quite a good collection for initial tests, these being as follows:

Aconite nap.	Ignatia
Aesculus hip.	Ipecac.
Anacardium	Lachesis
Arnica	Lycopodium
Arsenic alb.	Natrum mur.
Arsenic iod.	Nux vomica
Baptisia	Podophyllum
Belladonna	Pulsatilla
Bryonia	Rhus tox.
Calcarea carb.	Ruta
Carbo veg.	Sabadilla
Causticum	Sepia
Cinnamon	Silica
Gelsemium	Staphisagria
Hepar sulph.	Sulphur

If the beginner decides at first to restrict himself to one potency, I suggest that the sixth centesimal is the best all-round potency for him to use. Later he will want to acquire some of the 3x potencies, and to begin with he might select Arnica, Baptisia, Calcarea carb., Carbo veg., Causticum, Gelsemium, Hepar sulph., Lycopodium, Nux vom., Pulsatilla, Rhus tox. and Silica. At a later stage he will need 30c remedies and may finally wish to carry out tests with remedies in 200 and CM potencies. But the use of these high potencies should be prescribed only by fully competent and experienced homoeopaths. In any case they should be checked first, if possible, through radiesthesia.

Having once acquired a set of remedies, the beginner can proceed to test them out with only the addition of a pendulum and a 100cm. rule. If he places a saliva specimen, which may be his own or someone else's, on the 0cm. mark, he should (as we already know) find a balance point at approximately 38cm. By putting a remedy alongside the specimen on a rubber block, he will probably find the reading increases to 50cm. or more. A very good remedy may take the pendulum right up to 80cm., or above. He may find this second balance point easiest by starting at 100cm. and moving his pendulum slowly down the rule. He should then feel a resistance at, or near, the correct balance point. A reading of 70cm. is a good indication, and two or three remedies placed together alongside the specimen, each of which by itself gives a reading of between 65 and 70cm., may quite easily take the pendulum up to 80, 90, or even 100cm. When this happens the owner of the specimen should receive benefit, perhaps very considerable benefit, by taking the remedies. By trying out this very simple method of testing, a budding radiesthetist and homoeopath should soon become convinced of the value and validity of the homoeopathic remedy.

If the beginner decides he wants to acquire the Schüssler salts, these are generally prescribed in the 6x potency. At the same time, when drugs of different potencies are prescribed together, it is important to maintain a correct balance between the different potencies. Thus I should choose 6c or 12, 30 and higher (if necessary) potencies to go with 3x remedies, but not 6x. If the Schüssler salts are given by themselves, the practitioner may choose the 6x potency. But if a prescription includes 3x and 6c (or higher) potency remedies, the addition of a Schüssler remedy might well be of 6c potency. There is a good deal to be said therefore in having the Schüssler salts in both 6x and 6c potencies. Higher potencies could be added later. My list of thirty remedies already includes two Schüssler salts, viz. Natrum mur. and Silica. In treating a case final choice of potency must, of course, always be checked by pendulum testing.

Supposing that we test a 30c nosode against the specimen on the rule, as described above, and obtain a reading of 60cm. or more, we can assume that the owner of the specimen is infected with the pathogen represented by the nosode. If we now place a remedy alongside the specimen, but on the opposite side to where the nosode is, a reading may be obtained of below 10cm. When this occurs, the remedy is cutting out the waveform of the disease condition in the specimen and is suitable for eliminating the pathogen from the patient as represented by it. Any nosode giving a reading of over 50cm. suggests the likely presence of the pathogen in the patient, and a reading of 60cm. or more indicates that treatment of the pathogen is definitely required.

While the nosode itself could be employed as a remedy, the practitioner will generally prefer to employ a remedy, which has the advantage of having a wider field of action than the nosode. More-over, the correct potency of the remedy is easily found, while the practitioner may quite possibly have only one potency of the nosode in his possession. In any case nosodes are seldom, if ever, prescribed in potencies lower than 30c. The best course for the practitioner new to homoeopathy would undoubtedly be to restrict himself to ordinary homoeopathic remedies.

Provided that the practitioner has the necessary aptitude for this particular kind of test, he will find it simple to use and giving a high degree of accuracy.

Tests for Infection

An attraction of medical radiesthesia is that techniques employed by the pendulist never stand still. As experience grows there will always be times when the radiesthetist finds new ways of doing things, new approaches to particular problems, and modifications, however slight, to individual techniques. From small beginnings he will find as he goes along that methods which he could not follow himself, but were employed by others, suddenly become available to him. It can happen that one stumbles quite unexpectedly on a way of doing things which one had never contemplated, but which give better results than what one had done before.

I have described in this book how I found that 45 cm. on my rule was a natural point for testing disease conditions, and how that my readings above 45 cm. represented a positive reaction, I have since found that better indications for disease conditions could be obtained at the left-hand end of the rule. Thus, if I put up a disease condition on the radionic instrument at the right-hand end of the rule, connected to the 100cm. point by my vial arrangement, with the patient's specimen at 0cm., a positive reading would be anything above 10cm., whereas a negative reading would be under 10cm., and perhaps going down to the bottom of the rule where no resistance was felt at all. Thus, supposing I wanted to test a specimen for uric acid, which can be regarded as an indication of infection, I gave the rate of 0·41 for uric acid in the first edition of this book, which of course is not a disease rate, but that of the acid itself. As a disease rate, I found by my own testing that the rate was 40·41.

If we put this rate on the instrument, we can get a reading well below 10cm. at the left-hand end of the rule, or we may get a reading of 15 to 20cm. In the latter case the patient must be toxic and a similar reading might easily be obtained for urea. In a similar manner we can test an organ for inflammation or deficient function at the left-hand end of the rule. If we put up the rate of an organ such as the liver, we will probably get a reading of 48/49cm. if it is healthy, or one as low as 45cm. if it is badly infected. But another way of assessing its condition and probably a better one, is to take a reading in the 10cm. range with the deficiency rate of 10 set on the first dial.

Readings of 15cm. or more would indicate functional deficiency, while with those of 10cm. or under we could assume that the organ was fully active. Readings up to 20cm. can quite easily be obtained when testing a badly affected organ for inflammation with the organ rate on the instrument preceded by the rate for inflammation (which is 40) on the first dial, i.e. that indicating disease.

I should like to say a word about testing an organ on the triangle. Supposing we are testing the heart. With the patient's specimen at A and the heart witness at B (see Chap. 5), the pendulum should oscillate along CD if there is nothing wrong with the heart. For such tests I usually place S at C, which helps to stabilise the reading. If the heart is affected, as for instance by some infection, it will probably give a reading of 10 to 20° to the right of CD (or left in the case of a right-handed operator with the blood smear or saliva specimen and heart witness changed over to opposite sides). If heart function is badly disturbed, I may get a reading to the left of CD, and if I replace S by P at C, the reading may be to the right of CD. In this case I should say that the heart has a split polarity. S and P can give different readings indicating a split polarity, or they may give the same readings on either side of CD. For myself I regard the more normal readings to the right of CD (i.e. with a left-handed operator) as negative and those to the left as positive. I should say that positive readings indicate inflammation or toxaemia. What they do mean is that the organ is in a badly disturbed state, being badly out of balance. If one is at all doubtful about the condition of an organ, it is always advisable to test it on both S and P. Supposing one obtains readings of 20° positive for an organ for both S and P, an appropriate remedy should bring the readings down to, say, 20° negative.

One method of testing a remedy for suitability is to place it in radiative contact with S at B, i.e. with the sympathetic nervous system. A good remedy should produce a reading of 10° rather than oscillation along CD. This is what I find and I think it is because an oscillation along CD may mean that the nervous system of the patient would be somewhat over-stimulated by the remedy. In testing a remedy for an organ or disease condition with the witness at B, I now place the remedy actually on the circumference of the circle close to the witness.

Since this book was first published several new nosodes have become available and I worked out remedies which should deal effectively with the diseases they represent as being additional to the tables previously published. The results are as follows:

Brucella abortus—Formica, Graphites, Iodum, Phytolacca, Rhus tox.

Brucella mellitensis—Arsenic iod., Elaps cor., Graphites, Silica, Sulphur.

B. Friedlander—Calc carb., Crotalus, Kali phos., Staphisagria.

Influenza virus A2 (Hong Kong) (1968)—Aconite n., Arsenic iod., Kali mur., Kali phos.

B. Pyocyaneous—Calc. sulph., Kali nit., Ipecac., Lapis albus, Magnesium phos.

Typhimurium—Calc. carb., Causticum, Crotalus, Kali phos., Staphisagria.

T.B. Aviaire—Chinin. sulph., Drosera, Elaps cor., Magnesium phos., Pulsatilla, Stannum met.

The following are a few miscellaneous rates, additional to those previously given, which may be useful, derived from witnesses and nosodes.

Cerebral substance	3712
Spinal marrow	7314
Joint articulation	8421
Striated muscle	420
Non-striated muscle	2211
Male	4420
Female	4412
Water	3222 (?)
Influenza virus Hong Kong	4032
Influenza and common cold	30233
Ditto with virus Hong Kong	30202
Encephalitis	4032
Paratyphoid A	3023
Paratyphoid B	3021
Pneumonia (nosode)	4024
B. Pyocyaneous	5023
B. Friedlander	4072
T.B. Aviaire	4033
Koch residue	3031
Aorta, atheroma	3011
Myocardial sclerosis	3013

Colour frequencies

It was after a visit to Dr. Geo. Laurence that I decided to make a table of diseases according to their affinity with the colours of the spectrum. The advantage of this is that it can greatly reduce the number of tests needed to determine the infection, or infections, from which a patient is suffering. For this you test each colour on the triangle in the same way as you test your patient for a specific virus or microbe. If the patient is not suffering from any infections listed under a particular colour, that colour should balance against the patient's specimen at 0° on the triangle. But if a reading of, say, 20° is found for a particular colour, it is certain that the patient has contracted one of the diseases or infections coming under that colour. It is for the operator to identify which infection, or infections, listed under that colour from which the patient is suffering.

I used coloured ribbons in making up my list, and the results obtained may not agree entirely with the lists of other radiesthetists using their own colour samples. Nevertheless, I have no reason to think that my own list should not prove useful to radiesthetists who have not made their own lists based on their own colour samples.

In order to list the various disease samples or witnesses according to their colour frequencies, I placed the disease nosode or witness at A on the triangle and the colour samples at B, first with S and then P at C. If the pendulum balanced in each case along CD, I concluded that the disease witness and colour sample were in tune, or syntonised with each other, the disease being duly listed under its respective colour. The following is the table which I have used myself:

Red—Anthrax, Influenza Asian, Cold, B. Coli, Denys, Faecalis, Herpes Simplex, Herpes Zoster, B. Hodgkini, Internal parasites, Koch residue, Meningococcus, Mucobacter, Psorinum, Septicaemia, Strep. haemolyticus, T.A.B.C., B. Typhosus coli.

Orange—Bronchisepticus, Corynebacterium coryzae, H. Influenza, Lueticum, Medorrhinum, Morbillinum, Pre-cancers, Sarcoma, Strep. co., Strep. viridans, Syphilis, Tetanus.

Yellow—Botulinum, Calf diphtheria, Carcinoma, Encephalitis, Enterococcus, Erysipelas, Fibroma, Influenza Hong Kong, Hydrophobia, B. Influenzae, Influenzae virus A and B, Malaria, Marmorek, Parotidinum, Pertussis, Psittacosis, Rubella, Scarlatina, Soft chancre, Influenza Spanish, Strep. pyogenes, T.B., T.B. Bovinum, T.B. Meningitis, Uterine fibroma, Varicella.

Green—Appendicitis, Brucella Mellitensis, Dysentery, Gaertner, Gout, Morgan-Gaertner, Pneumococcus, Staph. co., Staph. pyogenes, Typhimurium.

Blue—Brucella abortus, B. Friedlander, Mutabile, Poliomyelitis, Pyocyaneous, Schirrinum, Staph. aureus, Staph. H. aureus, Sycotic, T.B. Koch, Tabacum, Typhoid.

Violet—Aluminium, Diphtheria, Enteritis, Gonococcus, Lead, Paratyphoid A and B, Pyrogen, Staph. abdominalis, T.B. Aviaire, B. Welchii.

Using colour samples in this way can greatly shorten the time taken to analyse a patient's specimen. One colour may produce a reading of 30°, while other colours may show readings of 0 to 10°. In that case any infection seriously affecting the patient is almost sure to be found under the colour giving a reading of 30°. Sometimes a reading of 10° will be found for all or most of the colours, and then we can assume that something in the nature of a general toxaemia is present and further tests will have to be made to decide the basic causes at work. I might mention here that diagrams alternative to that shown on p. 33 are available, but I have kept to the one illustrated as it suits my own method of working best.

Radiesthetists are very much aware of the part toxins play in matters of health and it is not unusual for a sick patient to show on test the presence of toxins relating to an illness which may have occurred years previously. Some toxins are hereditary, the most common of which are tubercular.

If we place a patient's specimen at A on the triangle and the witness for influenza at B during an attack of the disease, we may get a reading of 30° or more. As the condition is treated, the reading will gradually go back to 0°. But that does not necessarily mean that the influenza toxins have been eliminated. On placing a potency of Psorinum on the circle close to the influenza witness, in all probability the pendulum will again depart from the N–S position at 0° and produce a reading of 10, 20, 30° or more. This is a measure of the toxins left in the patient's system. A remedy must then be found, whether it is the original influenza remedy or not, which will return the pendulum to the normal balance point at 0°.

A word may not be out of place on the subject of 3x remedies. Many homoeopaths use 3x remedies only rarely, if at all. Nevertheless, I think they can be useful in reinforcing the action of remedies prescribed in higher potency. It may be best to take an example of what I mean.

Supposing that it has been decided to prescribe Cinnamon 6 and Rhus tox 6 taken together. If we place them together at the 100cm. mark on our rule with S in radiative contact with them and with the patient's specimen at 0cm., and they are well suited to the patient, a reading of anything under 10cm. will be obtained. This is really what I have previously described as a deficiency test. If a remedy is constitutionally right for a patient at the moment of test, its radiation is deficient in the patient. As the patient is treated with the remedy, the pendulum balance point will increase gradually to, say, 25cm., when it may be no longer indicated.

To revert to the prescription of Cinnamon 6 and Rhus tox 6, if constitutionally correct at the moment of test, they will give a deficiency reading of, say, 5cm. Now, with the two remedies at 100cm. on the rule and in radiative contact with S, we can bring several 3x remedies in turn adjacent to the patient's specimen, one or two of which are almost certain to increase the pendulum reading to 20cm. or more. In that case they are reinforcing the action of the Cinnamon and Rhus tox, but they are also treating the patient at the tissue or material level, and this can enhance the value of the treatment. A certain amount of food material passes through the body each day and this can be contaminated to whatever extent by virus or bacterial infection. It is my contention that the toxins thus produced can often be treated more effectively if the prescription includes 3x remedies. An advantage of finding 3x remedies in this way is that one or more may come up which one would never have expected. For instance, in an actual case of treatment with Cinnamon 6 and Rhus tox 6, the only remedy of the several tested that proved compatible was Lycopodium 3x. Further tests confirmed the value of this remedy in the prescription.

It is not necessary to test any great number of 3x remedies. Out of a dozen or so of the more common remedies, one or two will in all probability be found to go into the prescription. If more than two remedies are found in this way, they can be tested against the rate for toxins, which should make it easier to decide on the final choice, which one would normally want to restrict to not more than two remedies.

Remedies selected in this way may well bear no clear relation to the higher potency remedies, as already indicated, but they should help the patient towards recovery. They obviously cover some disease process in the patient's body that needs attention. On the other hand there will often be obvious links between the 3x remedies and the higher potency remedies occurring in the prescription. To take an example. Where a remedy employed in 6c or higher potency is Calcarea sulph. (one of our most important remedies), a 3x remedy which is almost sure to reinforce its action is Hepar sulph. Sometimes a remedy is only available in potencies of 6c or above, and it is obviously an advantage if one can find a 3x remedy other than itself to reinforce its action. In actual testing, often enough it will be found that a 3x remedy will do little or nothing to add to the effect of the same remedy in higher potency.

Dr. Guyon Richards was a believer in 3x remedies and I can testify to the value of his prescriptions on this count. Often enough, if one feels one has had enough of the higher potency remedies, one can continue very comfortably by restricting oneself to the 3x remedies. On the triangle it may be found that the correct 3x remedies will seemingly deal with the actual infections, but in fact it will be the toxins of the disease rather than the disease itself which they are mainly attacking.

New polarity test

It is only comparatively recently that I have employed a technique for testing the polarity of a patient on the triangle. In this case I place the patient's specimen at A, and S and P in turn at C. If the pendulum balances at 0°, there is not very much wrong with the patient, which is not to say that he is completely free of any infection. He is not acutely ill. But if his system is badly affected by some pathogen, whether virus or bacterium, the pendulum will depart from the normal N–S balance point when tested on S or P, and quite probably on both if the infection is sufficiently acute.

If a remedy placed close to A restores the pendulum balance point to 0°, that remedy is well indicated and we may say that it is constitutional to the patient at the moment of testing. That does not necessarily mean that the remedy tested is all that is required to effect a cure, but this is a very useful way of deciding whether a remedy is suitable for the patient and should improve his condition. If there is any doubt in a difficult case to decide whether a remedy is entirely suitable to the case under consideration, this test for polarity can settle the point and may be used also to make sure that the right potency is employed. This test for polarity on the triangle should not be confused with the polarity test employed on the rule, which is something quite different. Each has its uses. I have sometimes found that another test for suitability is to see what effect the remedy has on the pituitary gland. In any indisposition or sickness the pituitary gland is almost always affected.

Of all the nasty infections with which the practitioner has to deal, that of a tape worm is among the most unpleasant, and it is not always an easy matter to ensure its complete elimination. I have recently employed a technique, with the help of the polarity test, for dealing with this situation. But to be successful one must have a rate for the exact type of worm involved. This can probably be found from the parasites listed in a radionic rates book or from the several parasitic Turenne witnesses available.

A very good remedy for the treatment of tape worm is Cuprum oxy. nig. plus Ant. crud. and we can use the polarity test to find out if it suits the patient. According to my own tests the correct potency is 3x and not 1x as is often prescribed in oral treatment. The remedy is fairly toxic.

If we place the patient's specimen at A and the Turenne witness at B, a reading of 30–40° is clear evidence that the tape worm represented by the witness is present in the patient. We now place a second specimen of the patient on one plate and the remedy on the second plate (or both together if there is only one plate) of a radionic instrument and put up the complementary rate for the tape worm involved. With the instrument properly tuned and connected to earth we are now attacking the tape worm purely through radiation, or what is often referred to as distant treatment.

After treatment has begun a specimen of the patient is placed at 0° on the rule and, with the vial connection to another radionic instrument at 100cm., the combined rate for death of the appertaining parasite is set on the instrument. A reading of 0–5cm. will then be obtained. As treatment proceeds, the pendulum balance point will gradually move up the rule until it reaches about 20cm. At this point we may assume that the parasite has been destroyed and it is time to stop the treatment. The time needed for this operation can be put at 30–40 minutes. Going back to the triangle we will find at this stage, when the rule reading has reached 20cm., the polarity of the patient will have gone out of balance, with the worst reading probably found when tested on P.

I have found this technique to be effective, but it has to be remembered that after the tape worm has been destroyed, it is very probable that other parasitic conditions may still be present and these must be dealt with accordingly. In one case I knew of infestation by thread worms was very evident. At the time of writing I have had little experience with this precise method of treating a tape worm, but I have referred to it as it may interest practitioners. It can avoid the more orthodox methods of treatment which are not very pleasant and not always easy for ensuring success. For myself I am satisfied that the method works.

Two ways of assessing by pendulum the length of radionic treatment in dealing with virus or bacterial infection or other disease conditions are as follows. 1. Immediately treatment has begun, find the vitality reading, i.e. the balance point on the rule with only the patient's specimen on it at 0cm., which may be something like 60cm. As treatment proceeds, the pendulum balance point will move down the rule until it reaches 0–5cm., when treatment should stop.

2. As treatment proceeds test the P polarity of the patient, i.e. with the specimen at 0cm. on the rule and a sample of P alongside it on a rubber block. Nothing else should be on the rule or in radiative contact with it. After a time the P polarity will begin to increase from about 5cm. and then on to 15cm. I do not think treatment should go beyond this point. These two tests are put out only as suggestions for pendulists wanting to find ways of assessing dosage in distant treatment.

Too much should not be read into the test for polarity on the triangle. A patient badly affected by some pathogen or disease condition is almost bound to show magnetic imbalance. At the same time normal readings may quite easily occur when the patient is debilitated. Familiarity with the test will help the practitioner to interpret the findings.

S and P may be compared with the north and south poles of a bar magnet. They may in fact be said to be the radiesthetic equivalents of the poles of an ordinary iron magnet. It is not without interest that the distinguished radiesthetist, Mrs. Barraclough, used to make double tests on organs by employing a small bar magnet, using it first at the base of her triangle arranged in a N–S direction and then with the magnet turned through 180°, still taking up a N–S line. I can remember her saying that two tests on an organ were necessary with the assistance of her small magnet, if a complete radiesthetic assessment of the condition of the organ was to be made. In the general run of radiesthetic work, however, it is hardly necessary to use the double check. I find myself that with the diagram I use, keeping S at C in single tests on organs does help to stabilise the readings and increase accuracy. Where the condition of an organ is of special importance, I use the double check.

A plea for tolerance

I should like to say a word about the method I use for diagnostic purposes of combining pendulum operation with the radionic instrument via the vial connection. My introduction to employing human sensitivity for diagnosis was through the pendulum. During the 1939–45 war it was impossible to obtain Turenne witnesses in England and, even with them, I realised what a great advantage it would be if I could use the rates as set up on a radionic instrument for testing. I took some lessons in radionics which proved extremely interesting, but I realised in the end that for me the 'stick' method of diagnosis with a radionic instrument was not very satisfactory. I could indeed obtain a 'stick', but not with that degree of precision necessary for ordinary work. It was then that I discovered the vial connection method of working, and this gave me all the scope I needed.

I am of course aware that radionic instruments generally have been designed for use with the 'stick', although at one time some instruments were constructed for work with the pendulum. And I also know how very satisfactory the 'stick' method can be in truly skilled hands. But I also believe that those who can use the 'stick' method with the necessary degree of competence are comparatively few.

A great deal depends on how a 'dowsing' practitioner is first introduced to the subject. If it is through a course of radionics, he will probably find the 'stick' method satisfactory—at least up to a point. The situation is entirely different with the pendulist, who can claim with strong conviction that the pendulum provides the most sensitive of all dowsing techniques. If the pendulist wishes to obtain information only available to him through a radionic instrument, he should be entirely free to employ it in the manner which suits him best. Indeed I should have thought that the orthodox radionic practitioner would have welcomed tests carried out by a method he does not consider orthodox, if by that method the accuracy and precision of the radionic instrument is thereby confirmed.

Dowsing (used in its widest sense) is a very personal affair and each individual has to develop his own special skill. Whether he is a pendulist or a 'stick' advocate, or indeed works in some other entirely different way, he should leave others to follow their own bent and ways of working. If there are any who would like to restrict the use of radionic instruments only to those who consent to operate them in one particular way, I should regard that as retrogressive and redolent of the Dark Ages.

Index

A general check-up, 58
A question of potency, 63
A Radiesthetic Approach to Health and Homoeopathy, 11
ABRAMS, Dr. ALBERT, 46
Agricultural Research Council, 96
Aluminium poisoning, 13, 69, 87
An Introduction to Medical Radiesthesia and Radionics, 10, 11

BARRACLOUGH, Mrs. GLADYS, 32
Blood pressure, 84
BOVIS, A., 48
BRUNLER, Dr. OSCAR, 48

Calcium deficiency, 37
Catarrh, 65
Chain of Life, The, 46, 128, 129
Colds and influenza, 60
Colour reactions, 16
Complementary rates, 93, 141
Cystitis, 89

Debility, 82
'Deficiency' test, 63
Delawarr Laboratories, 41, 72, 84, 90, 93
Diet, 85
Diverticulitis, 75
Dosage, 55
Dowsing, 16
DROWN, Dr. RUTH, 93

E.S.P., 43, 44

General Disease Conditions, 50
'General Polarity', 19

Growths, 77

Haemorrhoids, 13, 81
HAHNEMANN, Dr. CHRISTIAN SAMUEL, 143
Headaches, 68
Homoeopathy for the First-Aider, 68

I.M.R.R., 11, 17, 22, 38, 40, 90

LAURENCE, Dr. GEO., 10
LONG, MAX FREEDOM, 49

Malaria, 70
Map-dowsing, 19, 44
Medical Research Committee, 96
Meningococcus, 80
MERMET, Abbé, 16
Microsonic therapy, 38, 79, 90

Nosodes, 29, 30
NYEMANN, HARRIET, 89

Odic force, 49

Parasites, 71, 138, 139, 140
Pattern of Health, The, 49
Pendulum reactions, 16
Pendulum, choice of, 17
Polarity readings, 24
Poliomyelitis, 88
Psoriasis, 90

R (rule) readings, 22
REICHENBACH, Baron von, 49
RICHARDS, Dr. W. GUYON, 26, 32, 36, 45, 46, 84, 118, 125, 128, 129

S and P, 23
SHEPHERD, Dr. DOROTHY, 66, 68, 118
SMITH, Mr., 46
Streams, underground, 18

Tobacco, possible ill effects of, 87
TOMLINSON, Dr. H., 125
Trauma and shock, 66
TRINDER, Captain W. H., 16
TROMP, Professor S. W., 49

Turenne witnesses, 27, 28
'Twenty Questions', 48

Urea and uric acid, 26, 51
Uterine fibroma, 78, 79, 80

'Vial connection', 38

WARR, GEO. DE LA, 49
WESTLAKE, Dr. AUBREY, 49
Wrist, strained, 54